HINDOOLOGY
BOOKS

AF541133

Knowing
GURU NANAK
Prof. Shrikant Prasoon

Published by

An Imprint of
Pustak Mahal®, Delhi

J-3/16 , Daryaganj, New Delhi-110002
☎ 23276539, 23272783, 23272784 • *Fax:* 011-23260518
E-mail: info@pustakmahal.com • *Website:* www.pustakmahal.com

London Office
5, Roddell Court, Bath Road, Slough SL3OQ J, England
E-mail: pustakmahaluk@pustakmahal.com

Sales Centre
10-B, Netaji Subhash Marg, Daryaganj, New Delhi-110002
☎ 23268292, 23268293, 23279900 • *Fax:* 011-23280567

Branch Offices
Bangalore: ☎ 22234025
E-mail: pmblr@sancharnet.in • pustak@sancharnet.in
Mumbai: ☎ 22010941
E-mail: rapidex@bom5.vsnl.net.in
Patna: ☎ 3094193 • *Telefax:* 0612-2302719
E-mail: rapidexptn@rediffmail.com
Hyderabad: *Telefax:* 040-24737290
E-mail: pustakmahalhyd@yahoo.co.in

ISBN 978-81-223-0980-5
Edition : 2007

Dedication

Dedicated to those
Who wish to obtain
Ample Faith
Cosmic Awareness
Universal Oneness
Total Emancipation
and
Eternal Bliss.

Contents

Preface

During the late 1950s when I was reading in Marwari High School at Chakradharpur (Jharkhand), I had a heaven-sent opportunity to read as many books as I wished to because my elder brother, Acharya Vishnu Kant Pandey, posted there as a school sub-inspector, received books from the government for free distribution to schools and libraries. It was an office-cum-residence filled with books and magazines.

Goddess Saraswati blessed me with books and inspired me to read. Since then, I have lived with books all around me. It was Goddess Saraswati's inspiration that my elder brothers opened a bookshop and a publication which, within the next ten years, grew into three shops, two presses and three publications at Motihari (Bihar).

I became a voracious reader. Reading is my first pastime and second nature, and writing an integral part of my life. In the beginning, I read anything and everything I received. Later, when I became a Lecturer in 1970, my two senior professors Late Pt. Girija Dutt Tripathi (Sanskrit and Hindi) and Late Dr B.N. Choubey (English, Philosophy and Psychology) guided me, regularly correcting my writings, occasionally giving me select books and imparting invaluable lessons in the art of writing. Prof. Ramashraya Pd. Singh (Hindi) also corrected my writings.

My first poem was published in 1960. In 1965, I wrote a series of five books on Social Studies in Hindi under the guidance of my elder brothers.

Thus, I was moulded, formed and transformed. Reading and writing became (and has remained) a part of my inner being. I gave my soul to it. Gods and goddesses, gurus and guardians have showered their blessings on me. They have made me what I am today.

There is immense pleasure in reading, contemplating, composing poems and writing. It's always a sheer bliss. This is the blissful path I received and have been steadily moving ahead on it.

So, when Mr Ram Avtar Gupta of Pustak Mahal assigned me two books, one on Guru Nanak and the other on Sant Kabir, I was delighted. I accepted the offer and completed the books.

To write on a godly, legendary, spiritual preceptor and founder of a religion, Guru Nanak – an embodiment of piety and righteousness, compassion and truthfulness – is in itself a sublime task and a spiritual experience.

Now I leave it to the readers to read, enjoy, assimilate and follow his teachings.

—Prof. S.K. Prasoon

Source Material on Guru Nanak's Life

Right from the rishis, munis, saints and sages to gurus and poets, Indians were always occupied with their own pious deeds and the well-being of others. They worked for '*Bahujan hitaya*' (the welfare of many), and wished '*Sarve Vawantu Sukhinah*' (all should be happy). They lived and worked for others, the society, Nature and the Cosmos. Due to this, the personal details of specific individuals are not fully known to us. References may be found in the works of others, which form the basic source of our knowledge about certain individuals. Incidents related to their personal life, particularly the dates of significant events and great achievements, were least important in the eyes of detached Indians.

Guru Nanak was no exception to this rule. He was a true saint in the sublime tradition of rishis and munis who gave utmost importance to the Lord and least importance to their own 'self'. Rather, they surrendered their self to the Lord and declared themselves humble servants of the Absolute.

Indians consider the teachings of a saint, a poet or a guru as very important. They feel these teachings have the power to ensure peace and happiness; that is all important for them. So they follow him.

Guru Nanak, too, is hailed as a saint. He is honoured and worshipped throughout India, both by Sikhs and non-Sikhs. It's fascinating to analyse the sayings of the first Guru. He is first in many respects. It's claimed that he was the first saint to try and synthesise the best from both Hinduism and Islam. It has been forgotten that he was the first saint to amalgamate the essence of both *Sagun* and *Nirgun*, and to unite them by declaring that they are one in the Almighty, the Truth, the *Omkar*. Guru Nanak was the first to claim that the trinity of *Omkar* is actually *Ek Omkar*.

There is not too much of a mystery around the life of Guru Nanak as he belonged to the Middle Ages. He was the founder of a robust and healthy religion, Sikhism, which is full of ecstatic energy, tireless action and spiritual vitality.

Of course, all the details are not available, and all available material may not be accurate, yet a lot has been written (actually recited) by him, by his contemporaries, his disciples and by others who had faith in him. There are variations in these accounts that is simply due to the oral tradition. A narrative varies when retold or rewritten by another and yet another. However, one must consider these source materials.

1. The most reliable account is given by **Bhai Gurdas**. He was the first cousin of Guru Arjun's mother. His account was, in all probability, composed within

about 50 years after the departure of the Guru. Bhai Gurdas is a venerable name. It is difficult to refute his account, written when everything must have been fresh in mind.

2. The second source is *Gyan Ratnawali*, composed by **Bhai Mani Singh**. This is certainly based on the account given by Bhai Gurdas. There is some additional information but basically it is the elucidation of the original *Vars* composed by Bhai Gurdas.

3. The third source is the *Janam Sakhi* composed by **Sewa Das** or by **Bhai Bala** or both, in 1604 AD. Imagination, perception and prejudices are all an integral part of the writing. Bhai Bala's *Janam Sakhi* is claimed to have been written before the demise of the Guru.

4. The fourth one is *Nanak Prakash* written around 1823 AD by **Bhai Santokh Singh**. There is hardly any additional fact mentioned here. It's rather an assimilation of available material.

5. *Sri Guru Granth Sahib (SGGS)* is another vital source, but it mostly throws light on the inner self, emotions, intellect, reasoning and belief of the Guru. A sacred scripture, it is the most dependable source.

6. Different Gurudwaras constructed at different places related closely to the life of Guru Nanak are themselves important as they give other versions in detail.

7. The oral tradition is still alive and active. Indians have a way to carry over important traditions from generation to generation orally.

8. Lastly, there are numerous books and articles written by Sikhs and non-Sikhs; Indian writers and those of other countries.

On the basis of all these sources, the life of Guru Nanak can be comprehended and people from all walks of life and different faiths can be inspired to follow his righteous path.

Sikhism

Sikhism is a compassionate, humane philosophy and a way of pure and cordial living by interdependence. Sikhism is action for good living via the right means. It is a search for and merging into the Supreme God for oneness, freedom, salvation and bliss.

In practise, Sikhism is the religion of some 15 million Sikhs from Punjab who are now found all over the world. They have made *Wahe Guru* known worldwide. Sikhism is a way of living a pious, righteous life. It is an effort to create a balance between a physical and spiritual life. It aims at the purification of both the body and mind. It proclaims that truth is higher than anything else but truthful living is higher still (*Sri, 62*).

Sorath (*595*) gives an insight into worldly business and spiritual dealing. "Make your transient life your shop; and true divine name your only merchandise. Make alertness and purity your warehouse. Treasure the name of God in it. Deal only with the Lord's dealers: you will get a fair profit and remain happy."

Guru Nanak

Guru Nanak founded Sikhism in the 15th century. He was born near Lahore (now in Pakistan) in 1469 and merged into the eternal lord, *Ek Omkareswar*, in 1539. Some say he was a *Vaishya* (belonging to the Hindu mercantile class) and others claim he was born a *Kshatriya* (Hindu warrior class).

Guru Nanak showed a strong spiritual longing and prowess during his childhood in learning, debates, philosophy and dealings with saints, *fakirs* and Sufis. This continued to be the norm till the end. He did not wait for others to come to him. Instead, he travelled far and wide within India and abroad, and visited all the famous religious centres of each religion, most being Hindu and Muslim pilgrim centres. He was in search of spiritual truth. He tapped different sources and attained the supreme knowledge with dedication by surrendering his ego to that inborn, unseen Guru, the Creator, Almighty and Beneficent One. Guru Nanak used different words to describe the Lord but conceded that He is indescribable and "belongs to all and is for all alike".

He stands for everything, manifests in all and pervades all. He is the primal cause of all and has no cause for Himself. He is the creator and controller of this universe. He is free from birth and death. He changes all but Himself is changeless. That Lord is indestructible, immovable, invisible, omniscient, omnipotent and omnipresent. He is intrepid, just, merciful and the saviour of all.

Grace of the Guru

It is clear that for knowing and merging into the Absolute, the Grace of the Guru is essential. Therefore, the Guru is

Guru Nanak Dev

Guru Angad Dev

Guru Amar Das

Guru Ram Das

Guru Arjan Dev

Guru Har Gobind

the most powerful entity in Sikhism, which has ten Gurus. 1. Guru Nanak, 2. Guru Angad, 3. Guru Amar Das, 4. Guru Ram Das, 5. Guru Arjun Dev, 6. Guru Har Gobind, 7. Guru Har Rai, 8. Guru Har Krishan, 9. Guru Tegh Bahadur, 10. Guru Gobind Singh.

The Five Ks

Sikhism lays stress on keeping the five Ks: 1. *Kesh* – uncut natural hair on the head. 2. *Kangha* – the comb kept in the hair. 3. *Kara* – the steel bracelet worn round the wrist. 4. *Kirpan* – the steel dagger, sheathed and hanging below the left arm. 5. *Kachcha* – the short linen breeches reaching up to but not covering the knees.

During his long travels, Guru Nanak met all types of people – rich-poor, wise-ignorant, saints-sinners – and learnt different ways of social and spiritual life before he founded Sikhism. He treated all religious centres alike. In this way, he enhanced his awareness, enriched his inner being, tested his ideas, and weaved them into songs. Later, when he had attained the knowledge and had finally merged into the Lord, he founded Sikhism with his disciples. His search for spiritual truth was over. He settled at Kartarpur, where he attracted a large number of disciples. They would meet in the mornings and evenings for congregations, *kirtan* and *shabad* (word) of the Guru. The teachings of Guru Nanak are contained in a number of hymns, *Sakhis* and verses, composed and tuned in different ragas. Sikhism is the only religion of the world where all the teachings are in verse, melodious and available in their original form.

Guru Nanak is the most venerated Sikh Guru, who personally guided disciples.

Adi Granth

The teachings of Guru Nanak and other singer-saints and Sufis of the time, collected in the *Adi Granth* known as *Sri Guru Granth Sahib*, is the basis of Sikhism. It is the sacred canonical scripture of Sikhism compiled in 1604 by Guru Arjun Dev. It consists of thousands of hymns, mostly spiritual writings and teachings of other saints, poets and Sufis. Although Sikhs don't venerate images, the *Adi Granth* has become an object of worship. It is kept in every Gurudwara and all Sikhs – young and old, male or female – prostrate before it with covered heads as a mark of respect.

As Guru Nanak collected the richest ideas from Hinduism and Islam, Sikhism naturally combines the best of Hindu and Islamic ideas in a coherent way. The Hindu concepts of *karma* and rebirth are accepted in Sikhism, but the caste system and idol worship are rejected, just as in Islam. Sikhs believe that God is the only reality and truth; spiritual release can be obtained by taming the ego through devotional songs, and the recitation of holy names, meditation, contemplation and service. Above all, at each step the guidance of the Guru is essential.

Righteous action and right living is the key to Sikhism and undaunted faith in God is its essence. As Guru Nanak said, "Those who believe in Him, get to the gate of salvation, are saved with their kin, swim across and help others to swim, don't have to beg of others; for such is the name of God the holy one, that only they get to know who believe in Him. Recitation (*samkirtan*) of the name, *shabad* and *vani* is essential, as it is envisaged to be the only way to know and merge into the Lord, the only way to attain **Freedom, Salvation and Bliss**.

In Sikhism, the **'vision of the Absolute'** is well expressed in the opening of the principal morning prayer of the Sikhs, known as the *Japji*, immediately after the **Mool Mantra**, the **'Fundamental Creed'**:

> **Eternal the Lord; He ever was and ever shall be;**
> **Nothing is but the Lord; Nothing ever shall last but He.**

Core Principles

Two principles of Sikhism influenced the lives and conduct of millions: *the vision of harmony* and *the spirit of tolerance.*

According to Gurbachan Singh Talib, these two principles inspired the masses with feelings of amity, tolerance and idealism. There was an urge to strive for a society in which social justice and morality prevailed. Ultimately, people were inspired to achieve this by resisting and overthrowing tyranny.

In accordance with the teachings of Guru Nanak, the Sikhs believe in '***one primal Absolute God who is above all distinctions.***' This Supreme Reality is **Om**, the eternal, self-created sound, the purusha, the Brahma:

> **By Omkar was created Brahma,**
> **Who forever on Omkar meditates;**
> **By Omkar were created the mountains and the aeons;**
> **By Omkar was created the Vedas.**
> **Meditating on Omkar brings emancipation;**
> **By Omkar are the faithful saved.**
> **Contemplate, O man, the exposition of the syllable Om.**
> **In the syllable Om are epitomised the three worlds.**

Symbol of Om

Guru Nanak accepted that the three worlds are in Om and came out of Om but he never accepted the division of Om into three, the Trinity. He believed in one Om, *Ek Omkar* and created a symbol similar to ॐ, but different in appearance – ੴ – which is eternal and the most venerated symbol of Sikhs. ੴ is honoured and used by all Sikhs. As Nanak believed in oneness and one entity, he rejected duality. Duality has two meanings; Shiva and Shakti are treated as duality responsible for creation, Brahma and his duality fills one with ego, as one treats oneself to be equal to Brahma, *Aham Brahmasmi*. When Nanak claimed to shun duality, he meant the second one of Brahma, as he often said clearly, "Nanak is merged in Him."

The Anhad Beating

Regarding that eternal music, the *Anhad* beating, the Om, Nanak claimed that the universe and its parts play the tune: "The sky is its *tal*, the sun and the moon its lighted lamps, and the stars are the grains of pearls. The breeze from the mountains wields the fan, and groves of trees with flowers in hand are ready for offering. O almighty God, it is at such a moment that I hear the melodious drums of the *Anhad* beating."

Naturally, music is a part and parcel of the life of Sikhs. It's no exaggeration to say that Sikhs have a musical way of living. Music provides pure pleasure and adds purity to life. It is indeed the expression of exuberance.

Virtue and virtuous acts, morality and moral deeds are the core of Sikhism and Guru Nanak's teachings. He believed that virtue and morality are essential for success in life as well as in spiritual endeavour. Virtue is praised and virtuous ways are followed. In the same vein, cruelty, hypocrisy and vice are denounced. Humility and contentment, pure heart and mercy, patience and charity, kindness and endurance are taken as positive and essential components for success and happiness in life. The following lines prove that **'Good works are the sheet anchor of holy life.'**

"How shall you be saved without good work."

"Good acts are the tree,
God's name is the branches,
Religion its flowers,
Divine knowledge its fruits."

"O God! What happiness is there without virtue."

"Good works I have accepted as my spouse."

"As he soweth so shall he reap; human life is lost without virtue."

"Man ascendeth and descendeth according to his acts."

"Man soweth poison and expecteth ambrosia! ...Nanak, it is only the fruit of what man giveth from his earnings that he shall obtain in the next world."

Sikhism is a religion of equality, fraternity, co-operation, understanding, refinement and piety. Sikhism gives a positive outlook to life and fills one with positive energy.

OO

Guru Nanak

The first Guru of the Sikhs, Guru Nanak was an emblem of unconditional love and surrender to the one Absolute God. He had an adorable personality and an enchanting face; a strong, healthy and powerful body which always remained energised with Cosmic Energy and attracted others easily.

An ardent, enthusiastic worshipper, he showed strong feelings towards *kirtan*, prayer and the recitation of God's name. He asked his people for two things only: "**Faith and Love.**" He taught these values and filled people's lives with them.

Guru Nanak's book of verses, *Sri Guru Granth Sahib*, readily received universal recognition and acceptance and went on to become a permanent heritage not only of Sikhs but of humanity. The United Nations accepted this 'universality' by declaring *Sri Guru Granth Sahib* as a **World Heritage.**

His Contributions

Guru Nanak has been accepted as the ideal guru. Like others, he too addressed intricate social problems. He had such great success that most of these problems were unable to raise their heads for centuries. This gave permanence to his utterances. That is why people consider him to be a social reformer and religious leader who directed the immense energy of the downtrodden in a creative way towards self-improvement and self-realisation. He made them sympathetic towards others and developed their ability to survive under unfavourable circumstances.

In this sense he was a guide and "a sentinel of the citadel of society", writes Parsuram Chaturvedi in the *Contribution of Guru Nanak to Saint Literature*.

"The picture of the ideal human society that he [Guru Nanak] placed before himself was a thing of his own creation and he gave constant encouragement to those who helped him in the realisation of the same. Accordingly, in order to give performance to an ideal tradition, he summoned his able disciple, Lehna, and gave him the name Angad. Declaring him to be his successor, he went near him and without hesitating bowed his head before him. One good result of this action was that, like many candles lit from one burning candle, the status of all the Gurus who came afterwards remained high alike. Thus, all the Gurus of future became the same *Pravriti-Margi*, followed the path shown by him, and were always active to illumine the same, and make it suitable to the changing times – so much so that they composed verses like Nanak and gave themselves the name of Nanak himself. It acquired as it developed, an element of optimism born of the struggle-swept, energetic lives of the Guru Poets, which has become a source of encouragement to make our lives blissful."

Nanak attributed no qualities to God, he worshipped Him as *Nirgun*, formless; never in any physical or human form. His praise for the Absolute is neither 'ambiguous nor incomplete'. Truly in the spirit of yoga, he defined the ideal of life to be fixed on the Eternal:

Let the restless, impatient mind be fixed on the Eternal and find rest in God;
Thus will the Creator provide for man's union with Himself;
And love for the Eternal be borne.

He explained his idea with similes at another place:

As is the lotus untouched by the water;
Or the duck by the stream;
So, man fixing his mind on the Eternal
May cross the ocean of the world;
Thus, doth Nanak state the truth.

Guru Nanak discussed, explained and criticised most of the prevalent beliefs, both of Hindus and Muslims – much like Kabir – and rejected all that he did not find suitable for the masses or conducive to spiritual growth. He accepted, modified and taught some; particularly *Sahaj Karma* – tolerance, love and dedication.

Approach to Life

Guru Nanak had an accommodating attitude, a practical approach to life, and a special appeal for restructuring the social structure. His thoughts were much ahead of the times – an era of decline and decadence. He showed the power to effect desired changes in the minds of the people.

Guru Nanak reacted to social evils and religious taboos in a positive way, so he can't be termed a revolutionary though the subtle changes he brought about were no less than a revolution. He opposed superstition, injustice and hypocrisy in his own positive, determined manner. He claimed that by realising the power of the Supreme Lord and by reciting His name repeatedly, all worldly hindrances and hurdles could be overcome. Then the unrestricted flow of the Light of Truth would bring us to the Almighty:

By hearing the Word
Mortals are to godliness raised.
By hearing the Word
The foulmouthed are filled with pious praise.
By hearing the Word
Are revealed the secrets of the body and of nature.
By hearing the Word
Is acquired the wisdom of all the scriptures.
O Nanak, the Word has such magic for the worshipper,
Those that hear, death do not fear,
Their sorrows end and sins disappear.

Nanak knew ego to be the root of many evils. He advised people to throw vanity away. For him 'ego' was a disease. He pointed out that all sufferings spring out from the blind desires of men. So, he prescribed the following remedy:

By the saving grace of the true Name,
The bright and radiant Name
Of the infinite when it fills the mind
Banishes its impurities
And transmutes it into pure gold.

Nanak distinguished between sensuous pleasure and inner pleasure. They co-exist. There is hardly any difference between them for worldly viewers. He advised his disciples to seek spiritual pleasure:

Play truth and contentment as thy pair of cymbals;
Make the perpetual vision of God the bells for thy feet;
Make love for none but God, thy measures and songs
In this wise dance beating time with thy feet.

Guru Nanak was a true and sincere *Bhakt* who believed in complete and unconditional surrender to the Almighty who is the reality, and the truth. He aimed at total merger of the being with the Creator. He advocated equality among all living beings. He set an example with *Guru ka langar* – the community kitchen where members of all castes dined together, and *kartar* – showing the equal worth of all; and two Mantras: *Japji* and *Nam*. He explained an easier method of approach, *Sahaj Karma*, for righteous living. He gave a concise form to the morning prayer, *Japji*, i.e., *Ek Omkar Satnam Karta Purakh*:

There is one God
Eternal Truth is His name;
Maker of all things,
Fearing nothing and at enmity with nothing,
Timeless is His image,
Not begotten, being of His Own Being.

Though in his own eyes, Guru Nanak was a servant of the Lord, yet he possessed that unseen power that united the people of different caste, creed, cult and faith, gave them spiritual power. It was all social, political and religious awakening.

That is why he was swayed by the love of *Kartar* and from sheer ecstasy sang in His praise. Musical and eulogical words and ideas flowed out of Guru Nanak. Whenever he felt the urge he called: "Mardana! Tune the *Rabab*; poetry is gushing out; play on, for I want to sing."

There is no such religious leader who was so deeply absorbed in ethereal and eternal music. Yet, he did not allow any sentiment to go out of control. It was a disciplined ecstasy in him; even when he considers himself to be the bride and the Lord as the Spouse:

All alone am I in the wilderness
Lord, my Husband, listen to me!
How can a wife be free of care?
She cannot live without her husband,
Her nights are long and hard to endure,
For sleep comes not to her,
O Lord of Love, listen to my prayer.

He Showed Us the Way

For many, Guru Nanak was an incarnation of God, a physical embodiment of the Spirit. Some consider him a messenger who appeared as Light and dispelled Darkness. He showed the way to the otherwise bewildered masses.

When Guru Nanak taught the people, Sikhism was just born during a time of upheavals. People had no faith in one another. This time was quite similar to ours, with life similarly tilted towards the darker side. It's more deadly now because everything is polluted and arms are available everywhere. This is the most opportune moment to read and follow the philosophy of Guru Nanak for peace and salvation.

The world must be treated as *Guru ka langar* where all can dine together in love, peace and harmony. For this, one has to be humane, loving and compassionate. Today, with wars and conflicts on every continent, the world is badly in need of Buddhas, Nanaks, Kabirs and Gandhis, so that the chaotic, selfish, indisciplined world can see better human beings in place of selfish, self-centred ones.

A Guru Nanak is all the more needed for he had the vision to use various methods to unite different peoples.

ꝏ

Life of Guru Nanak

Guru Nanak was born on the 3rd of Vaishakh, Samvat 1528 (April 1469 as per the English calendar) at Talwandi Rai Bhoe, Nankana Sahib of today, near Lahore, now in Pakistan. His father **Kalu Mehta** (Kalian Das Mehta) belonged to a simple Hindu *Khatri* family. His mother **Tripta Devi** was a true picture of a traditional Indian housewife. His father was an accountant (*patwari*) with the local Muslim authorities.

Guru Nanak's childhood was different as he was totally indifferent to childhood activities. He had no liking for games, toys, clothes or food. He preferred to remain alone and liked spending time amidst Nature. He would sit idle and contemplate something unknown. That 'something' was not clear even to Nanak, but people suspected that the child had magical powers. He disturbed none for he was not like other children. He revolted against anything said or done to him which was not approved by his own heart and mind. The only 'objectionable' activity was his bold, ruthlessly logical answers to *pandits*, *maulvis* and elders. He would pose wise, witty, powerful and difficult questions with poise and quiet confidence. It was his poise that forced the elders to take his words seriously. They were not angry. In fact, a big, formless and colourless banyan tree was growing fast, spreading its roots and blooming in the heart of the future Guru "undetected and unclaimed", which caught the people unawares.

As a five-year-old boy, Guru Nanak raised serious ethical and religious questions. The elders were unable to answer these questions. He condemned superstitions at that early age and others simply looked at him in amazement. The dreamy child spent more time wandering from field to field or garden to garden, or walked with animals. He was restless and unable to remain inside the house or play with children of his own age group. Naturally, he had very few friends but they came from both Hindu and Muslim families, high as well as low caste. But he had no close friend. He was a lonely child. Naturally, he was unable to find a better companion, except enchanting Nature.

Guru Nanak was sent to the school of a *pandit* to learn Hindu scriptures and Arithmetic. Later, he was sent to a *maulvi* to learn Persian and Arabic. He had a sharp memory and agile mental faculties and usually learnt lessons fast and raised doubts wisely. Often, he questioned the very knowledge and authority of the teacher.

Guru Nanak was growing well in accordance with the prediction of Pandit Gopal, who foresaw his future greatness at the time of his christening ceremony. His name was borrowed from the name of his sister Bibi Nanaki, according to the tradition prevalent at their *Nana's* house (home of the maternal grandfather, termed *nana ka* or *nanka*). So, he became Nanak.

His father, Kalu Mehta, worked under Rai Bular who was a descendent of Rai Bhoe. Incidentally, he was the founder of Talwandi. They were direct descendents of Bhatti Rajputs. Rai Bular was treated as a nobleman of the place. It was just coincidence that Rai Bular himself became witness to many strange incidents related to young Nanak and also heard his highly spiritual statements. He developed a liking and respect for young Nanak. It was Rai Bular who suggested Kalu Mehta to treat the child differently. It all began when Nanak was asked to tend to the cattle. Once when he was with the cattle, they destroyed the crop, and a snake was later seen with its hood spread over Nanak's head. On another occasion, the shadow of the *van* tree did not move away from the sleeping Nanak. Rai Bular was a witness to all these incidents. The crop site is the present site of the Kiara Sahib Gurudwara, while the *van* tree is preserved near Malji Sahib.

Janeu Ceremony

Another important incident was reported at the time of the sacred thread (*janeu*) ceremony, when Nanak was just 13. During this ceremony, three sacred threads knotted at one point are worn by a boy. It is invariably put on the ears at the time of Nature's call so as to control the nervous system and save one from paralysis.

This ceremony was attended by common people and the elite alike. In the presence of the gathering young Nanak refused an ordinary thread and demanded the sacred thread. He sang the following verse or *Rag*:

Let mercy be the cotton
And contentment the thread,

Continence the knot and Truth the twist;
O priest! If you have such a thread,
Do give it to me.
It will not wear out
Nor get spoiled, nor burnt, nor lost.
Says Nanak, blessed are those
Who go about wearing such a thread.
(*Asa di Var, M.I. shloka 15.4*)

It was the metaphorical explanation that Nanak solemnly gave his family priest Har Dayal. He knew he had to mingle both among Hindus and Muslims; so how could he be baptised in one faith?

From thereon, Nanak began meeting saints and Sufis. But he was neither very close to them nor very far from them. He maintained a balance.

Ways of Life

Now his father, Kalu Mehta, was a worried man. His only son was breaking away from ancient family traditions. He thought over the matter seriously and decided to engage him in some business. Giving Nanak Rs. 20, he asked him to do business by buying and selling merchandise. Nanak enthusiastically headed for the market but at Chuharankhana he met some tired and hungry sadhus. He fed them well with the money and returned home empty handed but filled with inner happiness. When his father enquired about the business, he narrated how he had done *khara sauda* (perfect purchase) by feeding hungry sadhus. Gurudwara Khara Sauda is living proof of this.

It was too much for the father to bear. He punished Nanak for this act of kindness towards the sadhus. The site of the punishment is represented by Tambu Sahib

Guru Har Rai

Guru Har Krishan

Guru Teg Bahadur

Guru Gobind Singh

Guru Granth Sahib

Ek Omkar

Gurudwara. Despite the harsh family reaction, Nanak did not change his emotional longing and refused to be a man of the world.

Kalu Mehta had no option but to send Nanak to his sister Nanaki at Sultanpur. Nanaki was married to Lala Jai Ram, who was Diwan to Nawab Daulat Khan Lodi of Sultanpur Lodi. Lala Jai Ram used his influence and had Nanak appointed as a Modi to Nawab Daulat Khan Lodi. He was to look after a store. Even here, he behaved according to his usual loving, compassionate nature. He would freely distribute grain from the store. Once he could not count more than *terah* or thirteen (*tera* also means *yours*) when wheat was being measured. This enraged the Nawab and he was kept in confinement. Gurudwara Kothari Sahib stands as proof.

Marriage

Nanak returned to Talwandi. At the age of 16, he was married to **Sulakhani**, the daughter of Mulchand. The venue of the marriage is famous as the Gurudwara of Batala. He was happy with the marriage as he did not find it an obstruction in the way of his spiritual quest. The couple had a son **Sri Chand** in July 1494 and another son **Lakshmi Chand** (Das) in 1497. Another version claims he was married first and then went to Sultanpur.

In any case, Nanak had a fixed daily routine. Early in the morning, he would sing hymns in praise of God, assisted by his childhood Muslim friend **Mardana**, who accompanied him on the *Rabab*, a string instrument. Incidentally, Mardana remained closely associated with Nanak throughout his life and accompanied him wherever he went.

During the day Nanak would work for a living and in the evening he would sing hymns, while Mardana played the *Rabab*. People liked his songs and they became popular. Others now began joining the morning prayers and the evening ritual. He was on the right track and fast closing the distance between him and the Lord.

Revelation

There are two different versions about the revelation of Guru Nanak. One claims he went to a forest and remained there for three days. He had a revelation, returned back but could not speak a word. After a day, he suddenly announced: *"Nako Hindu, nako Musalman."* (There is no Hindu and no Muslim).

The other version claims that one morning he went to the river Bein with Mardana to take bath. He plunged into the river and did not surface. It was reported that he must have drowned as he was completely traceless.

After three days, he appeared at the same spot from where he had disappeared. He was a changed man now. He had had the revelation. He was in communion with God for three days. His eyes emitted the divine light and his face beamed with something strange and magical. He was in a divine trance. He did not speak a word for about 24 hours, then suddenly declared: *"There is no Hindu and no Muslim."*

To make his revelation clear, he praised the Lord:

There is but one God
His name is Truth,
He is the Creator,
He fears none,

He is without hate,
He never dies,
He is beyond the cycle of births and death,
He is self-illuminated,
He is realised by the kindness of the True Guru.
He was True in the beginning,
He was True when the ages commenced
And has ever been True,
He is also True now. ***Japji***

(These words are enshrined at the beginning of the Holy Scripture *Sri Guru Granth Sahib*).

It is the essence of the teachings of Guru Nanak. The *Japji* begins with an assertion that there is only one God whose name is Truth, who is devoid of fear and enmity, who is immortal, unborn, self-existent, the great and the bountiful. '*Omkar eva idam sarvam*' proclaims the *Chhandogya Upanishad* whose assertion became the basis of the religious philosophy of Nanak.

Spiritual Master

Now Nanak was a complete spiritual master. He decided to travel and propagate his revelation at the age of 30. It's a coincidence of sorts that three of India's founders of different religious, all based on love, compassion, equality and brotherhood, began their spiritual journey around the age of 29 and travelled to distant lands. They were Buddha (Buddhism), Mahavir (Jainism) and Guru Nanak (Sikhism).

All of them had their revelations in the lap of Nature. They had a very long life and *Purnima* (full moon night) has a special place in their lives. There are other similarities too which arouse curiosity.

Nanak took to extensive travelling. He would return to his place for a brief period and again go on to different places. There are numerous interesting events which took place at different places. At all places he was accompanied by Mardana with his *Rabab*. They never missed their morning prayers and recitals of *Sakhis* (hymns) in the evening.

He travelled to Amritsar via Goindwal. His halt there is testified by the Dukhbhanjani Sahib Gurudwara and the Ber Sahib Gurudwara. On the way he met a *thug* named Sajjan who later became his disciple. At Amenabad he stayed with the carpenter Lago.

Along with Mardana, Guru Nanak was arrested by Babur. Later, Babur heard their hymns and released them. On his eastern journey, he visited Gorakhmata. In 1529, he visited Achala Batala and in 1530 he went to Haridwar. These four great journeys are known as *Udasis*. After 1531, he settled at Kartarpur, the abode of the Lord, and undertook no more arduous journeys.

By then, he had established 30 *manjis*. These were local cells where his followers could gather to recite hymns and meditate. All such places later became Gurudwaras, which are now substantial in number.

At Kartarpur, pilgrims came from far and near to hear the hymns and preachings of the Guru. They rendered religious service in the mornings and in the evenings.

Guru Angad

In 1532, his new disciple Lehna approached him. *Lehna* in Punjabi means *debt* or *creditor*. Nanak heard his name and spontaneously said: "So you have arrived Lehna, the creditor.

I have been waiting for you all these days. I must pay your debt." Lehna was a great devotee of Goddess Durga. After meeting the Guru, he became his ardent disciple.

Later, Guru Nanak blessed Lehna with his *ang* (a part of the body), his hand, and gave him a new name *Angad* and said, "You are a part of my body." Then he placed five coins and a coconut before Angad and bowed before him. He asked Bhai Buddha to anoint Angad with a saffron mark on his forehead. When his followers gathered there, he invited Angad to occupy the seat of the Guru. Thus, Lehna became Guru Angad – the successor to Guru Nanak.

Guru Nanak spent his last days in Kartarpur. He worked in the fields to earn his living. He would give free food to all, Hindu and Muslim, rich and poor, who dined together. Known as *Guru ka langar*, it's still very popular and practised in every part of India on many occasions by the Gurudwaras and the combined effort of others.

Fragrance of Flowers

When Guru Nanak had grown old and weak, a debate began between Hindus and Muslims as to whether the body of Guru Nanak would be buried or cremated. When Guru Nanak felt that his time of departure had come, he asked his disciples to place flowers on both sides of him – Muslims on the left and Hindus on the right. He said that whose flowers remained fresh in the morning would get the right to dispose of his body according to their faith.

They readily agreed and flowers were placed on both sides of the Guru. Then he asked them to recite *Sohila*, the praise of the Lord.

Sing the praise of my Lord,
My fearless God,
Whose song of praise brings everlasting solace,
The appointed hour of marriage has come.
Come my mates and cluster around me.
Anoint me,
Pour oil on the threshold
And bless me
That I may meet my Lord.

After listening to the divine verse, he asked them to cover him with a sheet.

On the morning of September 22, 1539, when they went up to him and took off the sheet, there were only flowers. The body of the Guru was missing. Hindus took their flowers and cremated them; Muslims took their flowers and buried them.

Thereby began a great religion Sikhism and a lively tradition of the Gurus.

Journeys of Guru Nanak

One of the most important aspects of his life, knowledge, learning and teachings are the journeys of Guru Nanak. Though he tried to achieve a balance between the life spent at home and the part spent elsewhere, he spent more years outside Talwandi (Nankana Sahib) or Kartarpur.

His journeys have two different and distinct phases: One that he undertook for his own living and domestic or social purposes and the other that he undertook for knowing the world or making the world know him. In those days, journeys were not as easy as they are today but they were purposeful and meaningful. Journeys today are cent per cent mechanical.

Udasis

The journeys of yesteryears were meaningful, though tough and tiring. Guru Nanak embarked upon four different travels in 1499 (some claim his first journey began in 1505 AD), at the age of 30 when he was young and strong, and able to take the rough and tough roads, including varying climate and seasons, in his long and powerful stride. These four holy journeys are known as *Udasis*.

The First Udasi

The first holy journey was the longest one. He returned home after 12 years. On the way he visited Goindwal, Amritsar, Amenabad, Lahore and Sialkot. He went up to Jagannathpuri via Kurukshetra, Karnal, Panipat, Haridwar, Delhi, Mathura, Brindavan, Nanakmatta, Pilibhit, Ayodhya, Lucknow, Kashi, Patna, Gaya, Raj Mahal, Malda, Dacca, Dhampur, Kamrup, Dhubri, and Chittagong. He returned through the Vindhya region, Central India and Rajasthan.

During this long and tiring journey, he propagated his ideas and spoke before Hindus, Jains, Buddhists and Muslims. He delivered his spiritual lectures in temples, mosques and at different pilgrim sites. He spoke about liberation and declared that God himself elects his devotees. He talked about transmigration of the soul and rebirth. He laid great stress on internal purity. He led his disciples directly to practise *Simran* and *Nam Japna* and asked them to recite God's name: ***Wahe Guru***. He asked them to *Kirat Karni*, to honestly earn by one's physical and mental effort and suggested they share their wealth – distribution before consumption – known as *Wand Kay Shako*.

Guru Nanak stressed on *equality of humans*. He said, **"See the brotherhood of all mankind as the highest order of yogis. Conquer your mind, and conquer the world." (*SGGS 6*)**

He was more than just the founder of Sikhism. In fact, he aimed at the amalgamation of different religions. He told Muslims:

> **And when, O Nanak, he is merciful to all beings, only then shall he be called a Muslim.**
>
> **(*SGGS 141*)**

He exhorted Hindus:

O Nanak, without the True Name,
Of what use is the frontal mark of the Hindus
Or their sacred thread. (*SGGS 467*)

He challenged and rebuked both communities:

To take what rightfully belongs to another
Is like a Muslim eating pork,
Or a Hindu eating beef. (*SGGS 141*)

It was a great, fruitful and rewarding journey for common men, his disciples and the Guru himself.

The Second Udasi

His second journey was directed towards south. As usual accompanied by Mardana, Guru Nanak travelled as far as Ceylon. This journey was said to have been undertaken in 1506 AD, which does not tally with facts. It must have taken place at a later date.

Guru Nanak went to Ajmer and Pushkar via Sirsa and Bikaner, then to Abu, Ujjain, Bidar, Pongal, Madras (Chennai), Nagapattam and finally to Ceylon (Sri Lanka). The return journey took him to Rameswaram via the Malabar coast, Sudampuri, Dwarka, Sindh and Montgomery. He returned to Lahore via Talwandi.

When he was returning, he founded a settlement for himself (to be used later in life) at Kartarpur (which means *the abode of God*) on the western bank of the river Ravi. On this journey his popular hymns were accepted by a wide range of devotees. He declared that none can know His signs and accepted that "God's greatness is infinite. Ages have elapsed in discussing the nature, greatness and origin of God... Under the Guru's instruction God's word is heard, under the Guru's instruction his knowledge is acquired, under the Guru's instruction man learns that God is everywhere contained." He assured everyone that "They who worshipped Him have obtained honour."

By the time he completed his second journey, he was rich in experience and more confident of his goal of uniting communities.

The Third Udasi

In his third *Udasi,* Nanak travelled up to Tibet. In 1514, he went to Mansarovar and crossed over to Tibet. He travelled across the Kailash mountains and via Ladakh came to Kashmir. He also visited Riasi and Jammu.

Wherever Guru Nanak went he always wore a combination of robes and garments worn by Hindu and Muslim holy men. People usually asked whether he was a Hindu or a Muslim. His answer can be summed up in his statement to Sheikh Ibrahim, the successor of Baba Farid. Sheikh Ibrahim asked which of the two religions was the true way to attain God. Guru Nanak replied:

> **"If there is one God, then there is only His way to attain Him, not another. One must follow that way and reject the other. Worship not him who is born only to die, but Him who is eternal and contained in the whole universe."**

The Fourth Udasi

For the fourth holy journey, Guru Nanak changed his outer appearance. He dressed up in the blue garb of a Muslim pilgrim. He undertook this journey in all probability between 1518 to 1522 AD. During this journey he visited Mecca, Medina, Jerusalem, Damascus, Alleppa and Baghdad. He returned via Persia, Turkey, Kabul and Peshawar.

Two remarkable things happened in Mecca. One was his humble claim that God is everywhere. It happened when a man raised a hue and cry that Nanak's feet were towards Mecca. So he responded: "Good man, I am weary after a long journey. Kindly turn my feet in the direction where God is not."

Wherever one may be standing, there is no direction in which there are no holy places.

The second incident was a definite surprise for everyone. In Mecca, when pilgrims and holy men gathered around Guru Nanak and requested him to sing something, he sang in Persian. Before that there is no record that he ever sang in Persian.

The Final Udasi

After this, Guru Nanak once went to Delhi. In 1529, he visited Achala Batala and in 1530 he went to Haridwar. Between all these trips, he resided at Kartarpur. By then, he had already established 30 *manjis* for the propagation of his faith.

It was in 1531 that Guru Nanak took off *Udasi* clothes and settled down at Kartarpur. Hereafter, he undertook no more journeys. His worldly journeys were over; he now began preparations for his final journey which he undertook with celebrations on September 22, 1539 in the early hours of a New Dawn.

Leaves from the Life of Guru Nanak

Many famous anecdotes and tales from the life of Guru Nanak are told in different versions. There are variations in each version too. Different narrators and biographers mix and re-mix their ideas. The imagination plays an important role in shaping the incidents differently, often with differing conclusions. But the essence invariably remains the same.

1. Dunichand

The time and life during that period was definitely not what it is now. The wealthy and strong had their own peculiar ways of showing their wealth and might.

Lahore was not an exception. The wealthy there used to hoist flags to show their wealth. The variety and number of flags determined the richness of the person.

There was a rich merchant Dunichand in Lahore who had prospered well, accumulated immense wealth and had numerous colourful flags which fluttered high at the top of his large mansion. His prosperity was calculated in crores but the compassion, sympathy and kindness in him were at their lowest ebb. It was one way flow of wealth. He was getting and accumulating. He was not helping others and spending the money. He was a miser, not a charitable figure.

Once Guru Nanak was there in Lahore. He saw the attractive flags majestically showing their ego high up in the air. He was apprised of Dunichand's nature, wealth and miserliness. He wanted to teach him a lesson. He sent a letter with a piece of needle to Dunichand. The letter said that they were of the same age and were expected to die within a decade or so. As he was an honest and wealthy man so he was sending a pious needle for safe keeping. It must be returned to him [Nanak] when they meet in heaven after death.

Dunichand read the letter and looked many times at the smooth, bright and sharp needle. The question that cropped up in his mind was simple, "How can he carry that tiny needle to the heaven after death?" But he had no answer. He brooded over the matter. He was unable to concentrate on anything else. He could not throw the needle out of his mind. He thought and thought but found no answer. It was not easy to take a decision.

Along with the letter and the needle, as expected, he came to the Guru. He bowed to the saint and declared his inability to carry the needle to heaven, and returning it to the saint, he said, "I'm a merchant. I don't know whether I'll be accepted in to heaven or sent to hell, whether I'll meet you or not but one thing is clear, I can't carry the needle after death. No one can. You know it, and yet you sent it to me. What should I do with it?

Guru Nanak was prompt in his reply, "Dunichand, if you can't carry a simple and small needle after your death, then how can you carry all of your wealth after death? What will happen to it?"

Dunichand got the meaning. He readily prostrated before the saint, "Now I realise what you mean? Please tell me what should I do? I think I have wasted my precious life in accumulating wealth."

The Guru suggested, "Give ten percent of your earning in charity and ten percent of your time and labour to social work." Dunichand agreed and immediately announced '*Guru Ka Langar*.' It went on for months without break. Dunichand was a changed man now.

From then on it became an unwritten law for his disciples to give ten per cent of their earning and time in charity and to social service. It is still practised in the same honest vein. The service is done, the *langars* are arranged where people from all religions, castes and sects dine together without inhibition. The wish of the first Guru is honoured and being fulfilled.

2. Two Nights

Travelling was an integral part of the life of Guru Nanak. He learnt and taught during his numerous short and long journeys, mostly on foot. This was one important reason that he was closer to the masses and had a definite mass appeal. The experiences were usually sweet but there were bitter ones too. The Guru was neither moved by grand receptions nor disheartened on being ignored. One has to bear pain in order to enjoy pleasure.

On one occasion, he was travelling through small villages with his disciples. As usual, Mardana was with him. The sun was hot and the day very warm. In the evening they reached a village. Being very tired, they decided to spend the night under a big tree. The villagers were quite uncivilised and rude. They did not like the saint whose ideas were alien to them. For the first half of the night, they misbehaved in many ways. It was Nanak's tolerance and the discipline among his disciples that nothing untoward happened. It was one of the most miserable nights they spent. Anyway, the restless night passed and a bright morning dawned.

Early in the morning, they departed. When they were out of the village, Guru Nanak prayed to the Almighty, "O Lord! Keep these men united and confined to this place."

Mardana heard this and was disappointed. He wanted to say something but stopped short.

Throughout the day they walked on foot. The bitter experience of the last night was playing its part. They were not happy. In the evening they reached another village. They began preparations for staying under another big tree. The place was clean and the village looked different.

Some elderly people came and invited them to stay in a bungalow. The Guru accepted. It was a very pleasant night. Not only the place but even the people were different, civilised and cultured. The guests were fed well and arrangements made for their comfort and *satsang*. It was a memorable congregation for the first half of the night as people enjoyed the *namjap* and *kirtan*. Guru Nanak sang in ecstasy, Mardana played the *Rabab* and others participated in the chorus. The pain and fatigue was gone.

Early in the morning they departed. When they were outside the village, Guru Nanak prayed to the Almighty, "O Lord, divide these people and scatter them across different places!" Mardana did not like this. It was obviously a curse. His disciples felt sad that the Guru had wrongly blessed uncivilised villagers and now knowingly cursed civilised and well-behaved people.

Mardana could not resist asking, "O Guru! Why did you curse these gentle people and bless those rough men?"

"No, no! I have done nothing like that; how can I curse these kind, humble people. In fact, I don't want those rough people to visit different places, teach bad manners, and spoil the life of other people. They should not destroy the brotherly and congenial milieu elsewhere. So, I cursed them. On the contrary, I want these civilised, well-mannered people to go to different places to live, teach and change those places into better and worth living places."

Mardana had his answer. Guru Nanak was clear in his mind. The disciples realised the hidden meaning behind the prayers of the Guru.

3. Previous Life

Many illuminating stories from the life of Guru Nanak are recorded in Dabistan. They give insight into the life, mind and teachings of the great Guru. Some of them amply explain the Guru's reincarnation and appearance on the earth. Why did the Guru come to the earth? What was his purpose? Did he do justice to the duty given to him. Did he achieve the goal that was behind his rebirth. These and many other

Golden Temple

Fatehgarh Sahib

Gurudwara Keshgarh Sahib

questions have been answered well. Many small but significant incidents have been recorded in it.

This simple incident has far-reaching implications and connects Guru Nanak with his previous life.

In his previous life, Nanak was a very dedicated and pure soul who helped all. When he died, his soul came to an intersection. On one side was the way to hell, on the other was the way to heaven. He had to choose. Guru Nanak deliberately moved towards hell.

When Nanak reached the gate, the darkness around hell vanished because of his virtues. The miserable and tormented spirits in hell felt relief. Their pain was lessened and they felt comforted. The dark underworld was no longer dark. The gate silently opened. The ill-fated spirits, who had committed many unforgivable crimes, came out.

All the tormented spirits followed Nanak. They soon came to the gate of heaven. There was hubbub. God appeared and said, "These spirits are sinners. They can't enter heaven until they are purged and liberated. Your piety has saved them from longer miseries. They can now take rebirth. If they do good in their next birth and are liberated, only then can they enter heaven."

"O Lord," prayed Nanak, "then send me also to the earth to help them in their efforts to be liberated."

Guru Nanak's wish was granted. So, he took rebirth to liberate sinners. On earth, he liberated millions of men and women during his long stay. Even today, 500 years after his final departure, he is showing the way and liberating cursed souls.

4. Tera

Guru Nanak had spiritual longing from his early years. His father, Kalu Mehta, tried his best to make him interested in domestic activities, but Nanak was always on a different and lonely path, submerged deep in meditation and contemplation.

At that time Nanak was working as a store keeper with Daulat Khan. One day, wheat from the store was being measured. Guru Nanak was recording the measure. He began with *ek* (one), then *du* (two) and kept counting: *teen* (three), *char* (four), *panch* (five), *chhah* (six), *sat* (seven) *ath* (eight), *nau* (nine), *dus* (ten), *gyarah* (eleven) and *barah* (twelve). The moment he counted *terah* (yours) he lapsed into a trance and forgot its numerological value, *thirteen*. As if under some magic spell, he kept repeating *tera* (yours), *tera* (yours). He must have felt deep down that everything belonged to the Eternal Lord.

Others around him tried their best to make Nanak conscious of the counting but he was oblivious to everything. The work of measuring wheat was stopped. The matter was reported to Daulat Khan. Nanak lost a lucrative job and was punished. Gurudwara Kothari Sahib stands as a mute witness to this spiritual offering to the Lord.

From then onwards, Nanak did not serve any mortal master. In fact, he had already been appointed by the Lord to serve Him. He became conscious of this greater service. He remained a true servant of the Lord throughout his life: *Nanak banda tera* (Nanak is yours).

There is no doubt that Guru Nanak was born with a mission, and the unseen power moulded his mind and ways to such an extent that he could succeed in his divine mission.

5. Mecca

Guru Nanak claimed that all are sons of God and God pervades all. The Supreme Power is everywhere.

Almost each of the 974 hymns composed by Guru Nanak and included in *Sri Guru Granth Sahib* is a 'confession of the holy mystery, the pious wonder and the immanence of Godhead'.

This conviction of Guru Nanak is best illustrated through an incident in Mecca. He donned the blue dress of a Muslim pilgrim and went to Mecca. He had the staff of a *faqir* in one hand and the holy Qur'an in the other. At the famous shrine, he slept at a vacant place when he was tired.

A *mulla* (Muslim priest) noticed his feet were towards Mecca. He chided him for sleeping with his feet towards the *Kaaba*, the most sacred place of Muslim worship.

Guru Nanak was calm and gently requested him to turn his legs in any direction where there was no God.

It is said that his legs were shifted in another direction and when people raised their heads up, they were found towards the Kaaba. His legs were shifted again and again with the same results.

It was a miraculous sight and the onlookers were amazed. The wonderful mystery of the Lord was revealed to all who were standing around the Guru.

Suddenly, the priests realised that the man before them was a holy man. Indeed, Allah is everywhere and his *noor* rains over everyone and his sons and daughters have the right to sleep the way they find convenient and comfortable.

Nanak's fame spread. He concluded his stay with the following statement:

"Only those persons are true and good who have true love for God enthroned in their hearts. Those whose utterances do not reflect heartfelt feelings are false. Only those who are madly in love with God are real human beings. Those who have forgotten Him are a burden on the earth."

6. Teacher

Guru Nanak's father Kalu Mehta was not pleased with the unchildlike and serious behaviour of his only son, who remained alone and aloof. The father was worried. After a good deal of deliberation he sent him to a school where a learned *pandit* was the teacher.

On the very first day, there was a lengthy discussion between the bearded teacher and the gifted pupil. The teacher tried to teach him but the pupil refused to learn. The child had undaunted courage, appeared bold and wise. There was no end to the debate.

The pupil asked, "What have you read that you profess to teach me?"

The teacher said, "I have read the *Shastras*, the *Vedas* and the *Upanishads*. I have studied arithmetic also. I have been teaching others for a decade. I can teach you for another decade."

The bright pupil suggested to his learned teacher, "This is all useless. If you can get rid of worldly attachments and write but holy words of the Guru on the paper of faith, with the ink of meditation and the pen of heart, and make your mind the writer, if you can worship the *Nirankari God* who has neither a beginning nor end, then you can teach me this art."

The teacher was unable to fathom the depths of wisdom of his pupil.

A similar thing happened when Nanak was sent to a Persian *Maktaba.* He taught the *maulvi* what spirituality was all about and how we can remain pure and attain happiness and bliss.

7. A Snake

Guru Nanak showed signs of divinity from early childhood and was full of positive energy. The cosmic energy in a man is easily perceived by Nature, trees and animals, and are quietly attracted by the hidden power of a man like Nanak.

But Kalu Mehta was always worried about Nanak. He could not understand what was wrong with the child. In frustration, he once asked Nanak to take the cattle out to graze. The boy obeyed. He took the cattle to the field. As they grazed, Nanak sat silently under a shady tree and entered his inner self. He forgot the fields, the cattle, the trees and the crops. Soon, he fell asleep. The cattle were now free to move. They destroyed the crops. A Gurudwara stands nearby to tell the tale of the destroyed crops.

The next day, the richest man in Talwandi, Rai Bular, witnessed a rare sight. Nanak had taken the cattle to graze.

Like before, he left the cattle on their own and sat in contemplation. Meditation at short intervals was his forte. The pleasant, natural surroundings and the cool breeze made him fall asleep. Through the leaves and branches, a ray of light fell over his face. A cobra was attracted. It went up, stood erect and raised its hood over Nanak. The ray of light shifted to its hood and there was shade on the face of Nanak. The cobra's hood protected him from the burning heat of the sun.

Rai Bular was passing by and saw the sight with amazement. The snake slithered away when it saw a man approaching. Bular then took the sleeping child to his father, who was his employee, and admonished Kalu Mehta for being harsh towards his son.

The third day produced another miraculous sight. This time too, Rai Bular was a witness, as were many others with him. Nanak had taken the cattle to graze and left them unattended. As usual, he sat under a tree in contemplation and fell asleep soon.

He was sleeping under the shade of a tree. Time passed and the evening approached. The shadow of all the trees moved in the easterly direction, but the shade of the tree under which Nanak was sleeping did not move at all. It was truly a miracle.

How can the shadow of a tree remain static when the sun was moving westwards? A mute witness, that tree has been saved as a living monument and still stands near the Malji Sahib Gurudwara.

8. Lago and Bhago

The divinity of Guru Nanak lay in simple, pious living, in humility, tolerance, equality and brotherhood. That is how he himself lived and asked others to live in this rhythmical way for the peace and ease of the eternal music, *Anhad Nad*.

He had surrendered his ego to the Lord and was against those who had ego and pride. He did not like exploitation and excess by anyone, even kings or zamindars.

Once during his long, holy journeys, he was passing through Syedpur, Amenabad. Though the village was dominated by *Khatris*, his caste men, he had no faith in the caste system. He advocated and practised equality – a major source of power and inspiration for Sikhs. At Syedpur, he preferred to stay with a *Shudra*, Lago, a carpenter by profession. The Khatris did not like this. They protested and a group led by Malik Bhago went to him with a request to shift his *dera* (temporary abode) and stay at the house of a Khatri.

Nanak refused. There was a hot debate over equality and caste, fate and deeds, and labour and piety. A major part of the village witnessed it. Nanak declared that the Shudra was more pious for he earned his bread through hard physical labour while the Khatris were impure for they earned their bread by exploitation and injustice. So, there is milk in the bread of Lago, a Shudra, while there is blood in the bread of the Khatri, Bhago.

The Khatris raised a hue and cry at such derogatory statements. They felt insulted. Guru Nanak was asked to prove his point. He humbly requested them to bring bread from both houses. The bread from the house of the Shudra

Lago was given to Nanak. He looked at the bread, then rolled it in his palm and squeezed hard. The people were amazed to see milk flowing from the bread.

In the meantime, bread from the house of Bhago was brought and handed over to Nanak. He looked at it and repeated the same action. But this time when he squeezed the bread hard, blood oozed out.

Needless to say, the whole village became disciples of Guru Nanak. The Khatris felt proud to be the followers of the great Guru.

The incident had occurred when he was at Amenabad around 1499. Nanak was barely 30 then.

9. Karoria

Guru Nanak was returning from his second *Udasi*. The holy journey was almost over. He stayed on the western banks of the river Ravi for quite a long time. His morning *sumiran* and evening *sohila* became very popular. Almost the entire village gathered to listen to the hymns. Soon they started participating. Later, people from adjoining villages also came. He was immensely popular there and the subject of much talk and discussion.

Only one person was unhappy with his popularity – the richest man of the area and landlord of the village called Karoria. The land where Guru Nanak and his disciples were staying belonged to him. Karoria failed to digest the growing popularity of the saint. He decided to meet the Guru and ask him to vacate the land and move away to some other village.

He mounted his horse and rushed to meet Nanak. On the way, the horse stumbled and the rider fell, getting seriously injured. Karoria remained confined to bed for a week. This enraged him further.

When he could move, he mounted his horse again. Unfortunately, he met the same fate. This time he broke his arm.

After a month, he again set out to evict the Guru and his disciples from his land. His family members tried to stop him. They claimed the Guru was a holy man and should not be disturbed. But Karoria was adamant. This time his horse stumbled and fell over some bushes. Unfortunately, Karoria lost his sight.

Now he realised he was at fault and should not have tried to wrong a holy man. He repented his anger, hatred and jealousy. He sincerely told the people that he had no intentions of harming the holy man. He was led to the Guru and fell at Nanak's feet. He narrated all the incidents and sought forgiveness. The humble and kind Nanak forgave the landlord.

Karoria donated all the land to Guru Nanak and requested him to establish a village there. The Guru announced that the land belonged to the *Kartar*, so its name would be Kartarpur. Later, Nanak settled there.

10. The Rabab and Mardana

Guru Nanak was not only a poet who composed hymns but a singer too. His verses are classical in nature and outlook, not simple metrical compositions. To the purist, the poetic metre and the counting of accented and unaccounted syllables may not be true to tradition, but he had command of rhyme and rhythm. He compensated for the shortage of extra syllables with the *alap*.

As a classical singer, he had perfect command over different *ragas*. A lyricist, he may not be a celebrated poet but his perfection in *Sakhis* cannot be denied. It has never been mentioned when and where he received formal lessons in poetic and musical compositions. Perhaps he had no formal training in either of the two. Despite this, he composed as many as 974 hymns and sang them well.

These are the known facts. What is not known is the fact that he himself devised and designed a musical instrument called *Rabab*. Bhai Phiranda manufactured it. When the marriage of Guru Nanak was solemnised, the Guru gave the *Rabab* to Mardana as a wedding gift.

This *Rabab* is well associated with Mardana and, in turn, Mardana remained well associated with Nanak throughout his life. He was truly a devoted and faithful friend of the Guru. He served Nanak with 'single-minded devotion and unusual faithfulness'. An accomplished musician and a mellifluous singer, he became immortal along with his master.

11. Faqir Bahlol

Around 1520, Guru Nanak was in Baghdad, a stronghold of Islam. Oblivious of all talks going on in the city, Guru Nanak kept singing hymns in praise of the formless and limitless Supreme God. This was treated as blasphemy. The *maulvis* were furious and issued a *fatwa* that he should be stoned to death for his teachings. His utterances were treated as an affront to Islam and the holy prophet.

Without any fear or anxiety, Nanak continued singing his hymns. People who heard them came to the conclusion that the would-be victim of the *fatwa* was "*an embodiment of love and truth, humility and sweetness, compassion and contentment, forgiveness and forbearance*". They placed their feelings before others. The milieu then changed in favour of the Guru, understanding prevailed upon prejudice and revenge changed into reverence.

One man instrumental for the sudden change was Faqir Bahlol, who became a disciple of Guru Nanak and showed his devotion till the end of his life.

An inscription in Turkish preserved in a shrine at Baghdad dated 927 (1520-21 AD) claims:

"He spoke about the Hindu Guru Nanak to Faqir Bahlol, and for these 60 winters since the Guru left Iran, the soul of Bahlol has rested on the Master's Work like a bee poised on a dawn-lit honey-rose."

This historic inscription was brought to light and presented before the world in 1919 by Swami Ananda who showed "the piety, loftiness and lasting influence of that great man of God".

In a poem, Swami Ananda addressed the Master and wrote:

Upon this simple slab of granite Thou sit,
discoursing of fraternal love and holy light,
O Guru Nanak,
Prince among India's holy sons!
What song from the source of the Seven Waters
Thou didst sing to charm the soul of Iran?
What peace from Himalayas lonely caves and
forests Thou didst carry
to the vine-groves and rose-gardens of
Baghdad?

What light from Badrinath's snow peak Thou didst bear
to illumine the heart of Bahlol, Thy saintly Persian disciple?
Eight fortnights Bahlol hearkened to Thy words
on life and the Path and Spring Eternal,
while the moon waxed and waned in the pomegranate-grove
beside the grassy-desert of the dead.
And after Thou has left him
to return to Thy beloved Bharat's land,
the *faqir*, it's said,
would speak to none
nor listen to the voice of man or angel.
His fame spread far and wide
and the Shah came to pay him homage
but the holy man
would take no earthly treasure
nor hear the praise of kings and courtiers.
Thus lived he —
lonely, devoted, thoughtful for sixty winters
sitting before the stone
whereon Thy sacred feet had rested.

12. Shah Sharaf

During one of the *Udasis*, the holy journey, Guru Nanak came to Panipat. A renowned Muslim Sufi, Shah Sharaf resided there. He had heard of Nanak and knew his views, but he had many doubts. When he heard Nanak was in Panipat he invited him over and raised all his doubts. He received most satisfactory answers from the Guru. The important parts of that celebrated conversation are given on the next page.

Shah Sharaf: Why do you wear the dress of a householder and why have you not shaved your head?

Guru Nanak: It is the mind that one must shave, not one's head. To be humble like dust is the true way to shave one's mind.

Shah Sharaf: And what about the dress?

Guru Nanak: One must abandon pleasures and egoism and thus, surrender one's head to God. Then, whatever dress one wears is sacred.

One must submit to the instruction of the wise, while to cherish God in the heart should be the gown and cap of the holy.

He who controls his mind and relishes both pleasure and pain alike, and lives a life of poise and composure, for him it matters not what dress he wears.

Shah Sharaf: What sect and caste do you belong to? How do you live?

Guru Nanak: I belong to the sect of the right way. My caste is that of fire and wind. I live in the manner of the tree and the earth. Like them I endure being cut or dug into. Like a river, I care not whether one throws flowers into me or dust. Like the sandalwood, I consider that alone to be living which is fragrant.

Shah Sharaf: What are the characteristics of a *dervish*?

Guru Nanak: He is a *dervish* who, while living, is dead to the world; who is awake while the world sleeps; who covets nothing and has no pride, and who, having lost all, meets the Beloved, i.e., God.

Shah Sharaf (kissing his hands): Indeed thou art a man of God and to behold thee is to behold the vision of God.

13. Pir Bahauddin

Guru Nanak was once in Multan. As usual his way of singing hymns, his enchanting personality and Mardana's *Rabab* were attracting people. But there were some jealous ones who did not like this since their own fame and existence was threatened.

A Muslim saint of Multan, Pir Bahauddin, sent him a cup of milk filled to the brim. It was symbolic that Multan was full of *faqirs* and saints (represented by the milk) and there was no place for another. The indication was clear that Nanak should leave Multan and go to some other place. This was a time of political upheaval and unrest in Multan. It is said that only four things were easily available in Multan: dust, heat, beggars and graveyards. It was not congenial to peaceful living and contemplation on religion and God.

Guru Nanak thought for a moment and then placed a fragrant Jasmine flower on top of the milk and cordially returned the cup to the Pir. It was the most apt answer. Pir Bahauddin was astonished to read the sublime message conveyed through the fragrant Jasmine:

(*a*) Guru Nanak was as light as the Jasmine and can remain on top without disturbing the cup's contents or the other *Sufis* and *faqirs*. He won't displace anything or anyone.

(*b*) Guru Nanak was fragrant like the Jasmine and could live there just like fragrance. Just like fragrance, he would keep the surroundings pleasant.

It was an amazing but subtle answer to a very blunt question. Pir Bahauddin became a disciple of Guru Nanak and instead of bowing towards the west in prayer, he began bowing towards Kartarpur, the abode of the Guru.

14. Gold and Blood

It was the rainy season. Guru Nanak was staying outside a town. In the morning prayer only a few outsiders participated while in the evening hundreds of disciples came to see him and listen to his spiritual discourse. In the beginning, two visitors came to him regularly. But soon, one of them was attracted to a prostitute. So instead of going to the Guru, he went to her.

One day while both the friends were coming together, the one who visited the prostitute found a gold coin in the street. He was very happy to find this and went joyfully towards his destination.

The other one came out of town. He was moving leisurely towards the camp of the Guru. Inadvertently, he put his left foot on a dried thorny branch. A few thorns pricked his skin. It was very painful. He pulled the thorns out and somehow went to the Guru. But he was bewildered. He knew he himself was very pious while his friend indulged in all sorts of sinful activities. Yet his friend received a gold coin and God had given him prickly thorns only. He raised his doubt before the Guru and narrated the incident in detail.

Guru Nanak closed his eyes and contemplated for a long time. Then, the *Janam Sakhi* reveals, he opened his eyes and said: "Your friend was destined to come across a treasure today but due to his evil and sinful ways, it was reduced to a single coin, while – on account of your past misdeeds – you were to be severely punished today but as you have reformed, you were let off with a simple prick of thorns."

The Guru's insight satisfied all with logical and convincing answers.

15. Offering Water

Haridwar was and still is a great pilgrimage centre. This is said to be the place before the door of the Lord. Lakhs of Hindus gather there. During the *Pitripaksha* (fortnight of forefathers), devout Hindus perform *Tarpan* and offer water to their ancestors.

Guru Nanak reached Haridwar during this particular fortnight. In the morning he went to take bath in the holy river Ganga. A large gathering of Hindus was present. They were taking ritual bath and then offering water to their ancestors. They were facing the sun, taking water with folded palms, raising it towards the sun and slowly pouring this into the river. The same action was being repeated again and again.

This was a wonderful sight for Guru Nanak. He enquired about this and was advised that Hindus were offering water to their ancestors. Nanak thought this to be a foolish act.

He bathed. Then, turning towards the west he began throwing water. People were amazed to see a man throwing water in the wrong direction. Some tried to teach the correct procedure of *Tarpan*. Heedless, Nanak kept throwing water towards the west. A crowd gathered around him. His magnetic personality assured them that he was not a mad man. Then why was he doing this?

Some of them repeatedly asked the same question. Nanak replied, "I have a farm in Punjab which is very dry. I am sending water there to irrigate it."

People laughed at him. "How can the water from Haridwar go to Punjab?"

Now, Nanak stopped throwing water. Addressing the people around him he said loudly, "If your water can reach ancestors in the region of the sun, why can't mine reach my fields which are just a short distance away."

The Hindus realised their folly and fell at the Guru's feet. For many hours, he then taught them what to do and what not to do.

16. Perfect Answer

Returning home from one of the holy journeys, Nanak stopped at Syedpur in western Punjab. This was the time of the invasion of the first Mughal emperor Babur. War, killing, loot, destruction was happening all around and India was passing through a period of turmoil. Besides warriors, innocent people and children were being massacred. Human life had no value.

Guru Nanak was aggrieved to see all this. Mardana was also moved by the killings, particularly of innocent people. One day while they were walking together, Mardana asked, "Why were so many innocent people put to death along with those few who were guilty?"

Guru Nanak looked at him then turned around. He came to a banyan tree. He asked Mardana to wait for him.

He said that he would return after a while with an appropriate answer to his question. Mardana sat there waiting.

It so happened that there was an anthill where Mardana was sitting. After a while, Mardana was stung by an ant. The sting was painful. Mardana was angry. He began thumping the ants with his feet. He killed many ants, destroyed the anthill and was still busy killing them when Nanak returned and asked, "What are you doing?"

"I am killing ants," answered Mardana.

"Why are you killing them?"

"One of them has bitten me."

"But you are killing the innocent ones." Guru Nanak was calm.

Suddenly, Mardana realised that in anger he was committing a crime. He looked up towards the Guru who said, "Now do you realise why many innocent persons are killed though only a few are guilty."

Mardana had already realised it.

17. The Test

Guru Nanak had grown old and weak. He knew his end was near. So, he was looking for a successor to be the next Guru. He tested his disciples in many ways. Though he liked some, yet he could not take a final decision.

Once accompanied by his two sons and Lehna, a comparatively new but ardent disciple, Nanak was moving around his fields. They saw a corpse covered by a sheet. Guru Nanak asked, "Who will eat it?" His sons refused to answer as they thought the old man was not in his senses as his mind was elsewhere.

Lehna volunteered and announced: "O Guru, I'll eat it," so saying, he went near the corpse and gently pulled the sheet off. Under the sheet was a tray of sacred food!

Lehna picked the tray and offered the *prasad* (sacred food) first to Guru Nanak, then to his two sons. Thereafter, he ate what was left in the tray.

Now Guru Nanak said (quoted in the *Janam Sakhi*): "Lehna, you were blessed with sacred food because you could share it with others. If people use the wealth bestowed on them by God for themselves alone by treasuring it, this is like keeping a corpse. But if they decide to share it with others, it becomes sacred food. You have known the secret. You are my image."

Guru Nanak declared Lehna to be a part of his self, an *ang,* hence he was given a new name *Angad.* Nanak declared him to be the next Guru. Thereby, Lehna became Guru Angad Dev.

18. Punishment

From his very childhood, Nanak would begin meditating anytime or anywhere. He would then easily fall deep into trance. All worldly things would vanish for him. He was not attached to the material world.

Nanak served Daulat Khan for a long time as a store keeper. During such spiritual trances, he would give two or threefold more to buyers. Those jealous of his status and popularity, conspired against him. They were sure there would definitely be some shortage in the store.

They accused Nanak of misuse and embezzlement. Daulat Khan was duly apprised of the situation and Nanak was arrested. He was confined to a cell now famous as Kotha Sahib or Kothari Sahib.

Guru Nanak himself had no idea he had been giving more than what was required. In any case, the store's inventory was checked and found to be in order. Nanak was acquitted by the court.

Nanak was asked to participate in prayers at a mosque. Daulat Khan was also present there. Nanak went there and remained aloof. But when he was requested to speak, he exposed the hollowness and hypocrisy of the *Kazi* and the *Nawab*. At the close of his discourse he defined a true Muslim in the following words:

> **"Make mercy thy mosque. Let faith and sincerity be thy prayer-carpet, and what is first and lawful be thy holy book. Let sweetness of behaviour be thy fasting. Let virtuous deeds be thy Kaaba. Truth thy spiritual guide; charity thy creed and prayer and unruffled temperament thy rosary. Do all this my friend and God will bestow honour on thee."**

Daulat Khan intently heard him and was moved by his words. He broke his silence and said, "O Nanak, what a blessing it would be to me to have a *dervish* like thee as my vizier. Do stay with me. I have checked up my stores, there is no shortage there. People said nasty things about thee out of jealousy. I would not let thee go, now that I know who thou art."

But Nanak had other ideas and the greatest Master to serve and said, "Master, I value thy words, but no longer will I serve thee. There is another urgent call for me to answer."

Then Nawab Daulat Khan bowed to him and politely said, "I will not stand between you and thy Master. Go and do as thy God biddeth thee. I have seen in thee, what I have read in my holy books: the vision of God."

Then onwards, Guru Nanak became a permanent employee of the Almighty Master and served no other mortal master.

19. Sajjan

When Guru Nanak was in Multan he heard about a cruel Muslim *thug* Sajjan. The notorious *thug* lived in Tulambah, near present-day Makhdumpur railway station. He was notorious for poisoning those who passed through his area, and then stealing their belongings. Due to this, people of the area lived in fear.

When Nanak heard about Sajjan's cruelty, he was full of grief and decided to reform the *thug*. Accompanied by Mardana, he went to meet Sajjan at his home. It was like trying to tame a ferocious lion in his den.

People tried to persuade him to drop the idea but he was determined to do something concrete for the masses. Nanak fearlessly entered Sajjan's area. Nanak and Mardana were made captive and brought before the notorious criminal.

Sajjan was enchanted by the personality of the Guru. His words had some magical effect. Nanak explained the meaning of Sajjan's name, which means *a friend, a perfect gentleman*.

He pointed out the cruelty of his crime and concluded:

> **"Bronze is bright and shining,**
> **Rub it and it turns black,**
> **And a hundred washings can't remove it.**
> **They are Sajjans, they are true comrades,**
> **Whose friendship bears the mark of sincerity,**
> **Who are present in a friends' hour of need."**

Sajjan was able to see the effect of his cruel and dark deeds. He realised the futility of all that he was doing. His heart was filled with remorse and repentance. He fell at the feet of the Guru, and begged his pardon. Nanak was kind enough to teach him the first few stanzas of *Japji.* He showed him the correct way of gentle and humble living, which is the only way that leads one to God.

Sajjan awoke from his negative slumber. He was a changed man now. The Muslim *thug* became a saint. Guru Nanak was thus able to change his ways and guide him to sainthood.

20. Babur

This incident took place when the forces of Babur were in full cry. None was spared. Those who couldn't flee were mercilessly killed. Horror ruled the country. Anarchy, lawlessness, injustice and open murders were the order of the day. There was no one to resist all this.

Guru Nanak was worried. It was difficult for him to remain indifferent when human beings were being butchered on such a large scale. The young were hardly seen and the suffering of the old, women and children was difficult to bear.

It so happened that the army of Babur passed through his homeland. Along with his disciples, Nanak confronted Babur. It is said that they were all imprisoned. In jail, they began singing hymns. Prisoners stopped work and listened to them intently. Babur was informed. He called the Guru. There was a healthy discussion between them. As a result the prisoners of war were released.

Babur was obviously impressed by the Guru and asked him to impart words of enlightenment. Then Nanak solemnly told Babur:

Deliver just judgements,
Show reverence to holy men,
Forswear wine and gambling,
The monarch will bewail his misdeeds
who indulgeth in such vices.
Be merciful to the vanquished,
And worship God in spirit and in truth.

Babur was so pleased that in one of his rare generous moods he told Nanak to ask whatever gifts he wanted from the emperor. When the Guru declined, Babur pressed him to accept some gifts.

Nanak made it clear why he was not interested in gifts:

He who looketh for human support
Loseth both this world and the next.
There is but one Giver,
The rest of all are beggars.
They lose their honour
Who forsake Him
And attach themselves to others.

Kings and emperors are all made by Him.
There is none equal to Him.
Sayeth Nanak, hear Emperor Babur,
He who beggeth of Thee is a fool.

It was a great show of inner power, confidence, fearlessness, and devotion towards the One Absolute.

21. The Doctor

Nanak was an 'abnormal' child born on *Vaishakh Purnima*. Many great men are said to have been born on *Vaishakh Purnima*. Incidentally, all of them showed some abnormal tendencies. Their guardians were worried about them. At some stage in their childhood, they were treated for being abnormal. Some of these individuals include Gautam Buddha, Chaitanya Mahaprabhu and Rabindra Nath Tagore. Guru Nanak was one among them – abnormal, exceptional, unusual and unconventional.

A doctor was called to examine the boy. He declared that Nanak had unmistakable symptoms of lunacy. Unruffled, Nanak confidently advised the doctor to mend his mind and ways:

"Think of yourself and heal your own self."

The doctor was astonished at the remark and asked what disease could he, a doctor, suffer from?

The answer was ready and Nanak spontaneously said, "You are suffering from I-Am-Ness. Egoism is the worst disease in human life."

The doctor politely said he was primarily concerned with the body, its diseases and treatment.

Unmindful, Nanak prescribed a remedy that could change his life. He would be happy and never feel fatigue and moroseness:

"By the saving grace of the True Name,
The bright and radiant Name
Of the Infinite,
When it fills the mind
It banishes its impurities
And transmutes it into pure gold."

The doctor went away speechless.

22. Ahimsa

Ajit Randhava, a rich merchant, went to the Guru at Kartarpur and asked, "What is *ahimsa*? How can it be practised?"

The Guru replied,

1. Do not wish evil for anyone.
   This is *ahimsa* of thought.
2. Do not speak harshly of anyone.
   This is *ahimsa* of speech.
3. Do not obstruct anyone's work.
   This is *ahimsa* of action.
4. If a man speaks ill of you, forgive him.
   This is *ahimsa* of tolerance.
5. Practise physical, mental and spiritual endurance.
   This is *ahimsa* of energy.
6. Help the suffering even at the cost of your life.
   This is *ahimsa* of compassion.

ꝏ

Sri Guru Granth Sahib (SGGS)

Adi Granth

Sri Guru Granth Sahib is the most sacred and the only revered religious scripture of the Sikhs. Due to its simplicity, universality and stress on inner piety, it has been declared a 'World Heritage'. Despite the variety in composition, composers, ideas and *ragas*, it declares firm faith in one Absolute God and claims all human beings to be one. That one Absolute God is formless, pure, true and the creator of all. This 'Oneness' is the most sublime act of synthesis. The sacred scripture aims at synthesis and achieves it. It is the greatest and most glorious contribution of the book. The other is its "emphasis on the basis of equality and oneness of all human beings". It should not be treated only as a heritage but each one of us must try, honestly and sincerely, to live up to it in 'action, thought and speech', for making the world a better place to live and prosper.

Sri Guru Granth Sahib (better known via its abbreviation SGGS) contains universal, eternal knowledge and is capable of increasing inner power and making life easier. It gives the three most important things for a cultured life: sweetness, light and energy.

First Three Words

The first three words of the SGGS come from Sanskrit: *Sri* (prosperity), *Guru* (teacher) and *Granth* (treatise) and the fourth is from Persian, *Sahib* (master). It is a master treatise that teaches us and makes us prosper. The very combination of words indicates its varied content, its effort to synthesise and the aim to achieve greater heights. It assimilates the best from the *Vedas*, *Upanishads* and sacred writings revered in other religions. It contains the teachings of Guru Nanak Dev and 16 other saints, which widens its horizon and makes the symbolic meaning a reality.

At the outset, it must be clear that SGGS in its essence is the mystic word *Omkar*, *Aum adityam idam sarvam*, it is all and perfect. The only difference is that the rishis saw its three forms, the Trinity, and showed its positive, negative and neutral aspects, whereas Guru Nanak had no faith in the division. He claimed it to be *Ek Omkar*, ੴ, which means that the formless, or the one who pervades all is 'one' and absolute – He creates, fosters and destroys.

All the Indian scriptures, including SGGS, Indian wisdom and spirituality, takes its birth with and from *Aum*. Just like Guru Nanak, SGGS gets its light and energy from the *Anhad Nad*, the Eternal Music, self-begotten or unbegotten or the self-existent life-element or the Supreme Lord.

With that inherent eternal light, SGGS is capable of dispersing the darkness of ignorance, vice and sin, and brightening both the outer (physical) and inner (spiritual) selves. It shines on the true path, keeps it lit, and sweeps it clean of obstacles. It is self-light and emits light everywhere, easily and strongly.

Mystic Aum

Therefore, it is an eminent creation, distinguished and extraordinary, noble and elevated, illustrious and glorious, majestic and sublime. It possesses the divinity, vitality, spirituality and mystic element of *Aum*. It was the greatest act of collecting knowledge truly popular among the masses. Every element that has kept Indian wisdom and culture alive has been included in it. It has no peer and cannot be compared to any book in the world. It is an individual example and a class in itself. It fills each learner, disciple, devotee and scholar up to the brim. It has satisfied kings and saints, rich and poor, the elite and downtrodden alike during its formative years, and still satisfies the curiosity of theists and atheists and is capable of bringing in certain inner changes among atheists.

Recently, it celebrated its 400th year of existence. The reason behind its long life is its capacity to synthesise. It has *Mool Mantra*, *Japji*, *Sohila*, *Asa di Var*, *Amrit Nam*, *Prabhati*, *Malar*, *Suhi* and much more. The entire book is a collection of sweet hymns, wise *Sakhis*, verses of introspection and self-analysis, of immense faith and instant revelation.

The teachings of SGGS are not individualistic in outlook and attitude towards life. They have a socialistic embrace and as a result people from all castes, clans, sects and beliefs are readily attracted to it. It presents the picture of an ideal human society.

SGGS places the Guru next to only the Absolute. Without a Guru, none can experience the nearness and revelation of the Supreme Lord. All Sikhs, including the Gurus, followed and still follow the path shown by Guru Nanak. SGGS contains all that he taught and has been enriched with the *best* of spiritual literature.

The Eternal Guru

The history of SGGS, also known as the *Adi Granth*, began when Guru Nanak began composing and singing its verses and collecting his own hymns. When he began collecting the *Sakhis*, he knew the importance they would one day hold. By then he had established a few *manjis*, where his devotional poems were sung both in the morning and in the evening. The disciples there asked for more devotional songs. The need of the disciples must have forced him to work on the hymns in order to serve the Lord.

Even before he began this work, his disciples had already begun collecting them. Whosoever asked for them, Nanak obliged. In this way, the hymns remained scattered around the places he visited, safe with the individuals as well as *manjis*.

His successor Guru Angad Dev continued with the work of collection for he knew the importance of these devotional hymns. But now there was a difference. Guru Angad Dev himself wrote these in a new script – *Gurmukhi*. The history of the *Adi Granth* also includes the history of *Gurmukhi*, *Guru Vani*, Sikhs and Sikhism combined.

After Guru Angad, Guru Amar Das and Guru Ram Das were also active in this.

Guru Arjun Dev's legacy

The recorded history of SGGS began when the fifth Guru, Arjun Dev, with the help of devoted saints, disciples and wise men compiled it from 1601 to 1604. This included all the *Vanis* composed up to that time. The effort of the fifth Guru can be easily compared with the process in which the great epic the *Mahabharata* was written when Brahmarishi Vedvyas dictated and Lord Ganesh wrote. In the same manner Guru Arjun Dev gave the dictation and the greatest and most famous litterateur of the time, Bhai Gurdas wrote them.

In this way *Adi Granth* came into being in its first form that included the *Vanis* of all the five Gurus, selections from 15 saints and the songs of other Sikhs. It was really a Herculean task to collect, edit and give an acceptable form to all the hymns and songs scattered around many countries. But with the dedication of Guru Arjun Dev and Bhai Gurdas, this tough task was completed. All the hymns were composed in 31 *ragas*. This work is known as *Sri Pothi Sahib*. Its first *Prakash-utsava* was celebrated in Harmandir Sahib – now famous worldwide as the Golden Temple at Amritsar. Bhai Budhaji was elected the first *Granthi*.

Guru Gobind Singh's legacy

The tenth Guru, Gobind Singh, re-edited the SGGS and gave it finishing touches at Damdama Sahib. Bhai Mani Singh did all the writing work. The *Vanis* composed by the ninth Guru, Tegh Bahadur, were also included.

The complete *Guru Granth Sahib* is voluminous in size. There are as many as 1,430 pages. A major portion of the great treatise is in the common language of the saints – *Sadhukari bhasha* – the rest is in Sanskrit and Persian. Though it has already been translated into many languages, the scripture is not easily available. Thanks to modern printing techniques, though, it is not as rare now.

The Ultimate Guru

However, the real history of SGGS begins when the tenth Guru, Gobind Singh, placed the *Sri Guru Granth Sahib* on a high pedestal, bowed before it, declared it to be divine and sacred, and formally released the book for the Sikh community during a religious ceremony. He accepted it as the next Guru and declared that the SGGS was the eleventh and last Guru.

The collection of *Vanis* was not an easy task. When Guru Arjun Dev compiled the original version of the *Guru Granth Sahib*, the Guru's elder brother Prithvi Chand and others tried to insert some of their own compositions as hymns of the Guru. When this came to his knowledge, the fifth Guru was astonished and immediately realised that if such a situation continued it would undermine the solemn value of the SGGS and the Sikh religion in general. He knew the Sikhs needed an authentic compilation of sacred hymns. So he took upon himself the tough task of collecting the original verses. He called his trusted men and sent them across the country in search of the original manuscript. Prominent among them were **Bhai Piara, Bhai Gurdas** and **Baba Budha**. He himself made trips to Goindwal, Khadur and Kartarpur to visit the families of previous Gurus. He personally collected original manuscripts of these Gurus. He procured these from Mohan – the son of Guru Amar Das, Datu – the son of Guru Angad Dev, and Sri Chand – the eldest son of Guru Nanak.

After the collection, the arduous work of compilation was begun in a big tent by the side of the Ramashray tank at Amritsar. As mentioned before, Bhai Gurdas took the responsibility of the scribe of the master copy. When completed in August 1604, the **Pothi Sahib** was installed on a high pedestal within the **Harmandir Sahib**. The Guru sat at a lower level and instructed all Sikhs to bow before the **Holy Granth**, which was not an idol but the greatest book of divine inspiration. He declared that the divine book would remain open for all castes, creeds and sects. Thereafter, Guru Arjun Dev added the following epilogue:

Three things are there in the vessel:
Truth, contentment and intellect.
The ambrosial name of God is added to it.
The name is everybody's sustenance.
He who absorbs and enjoys it shall be saved.
One must not abandon this gift.
It should remain dear to one's heart.
The dark ocean of the world
Can be crossed by clinging to His feet.
Nanak, it is He who is everywhere.

Kartarpur Bir

After a name change, *Pothi Sahib* became *Kartarpur Bir*. There is a long story behind the change. It was kept in the house of the sixth master Guru Har Gobind. His grandson Dhir Mal wanted to become the next Guru. In order to put extra pressure, he stole *Pothi Sahib*. Some 30 years after the theft, followers of the ninth guru forcibly recovered it but Guru Tegh Bahadur instructed them to return the book. Throughout the 18th century, it remained

Akal Takht at Golden Temple (Amritsar)

Hazur Sahib at Nanded (Maharashtra)

Akal Takht

the throne of the Timeless One

The chief centre of religious authority for the Sikhs.

Takht Sri Harmandir Sahib (Patna)

Takht Damdama Sahib at Talwandi (Punjab)

Takht Sri Keshgarh Sahib (Anandpur) ⇩

in the custody of Dhir Mal's family. Once, the book fell into the shallow waters of the river Sutlej. When Dhir Mal recovered it, miraculously, no damage had been done. Dhir Mal's family was known as the *Sodhis* of Kartarpur. That is how it got the name *Kartarpur Bir*.

From obscurity, the holy *Granth* surfaced again in 1849. The British recovered it along with its golden stand from the custody of the Lahore Royal Court. On the application of Sodhi Sadhu Singh of Kartarpur, it was handed over to him in 1850. The *Kartarpur Bir* is well-preserved till date and installed for worship every month.

Banno Bir

There is another *Granth* known as *Banno Bir*. This is now treated as an unauthorised version. Guru Arjun Dev gave a copy of the *Granth* to Bhai Banno to take to Lahore for binding. Bhai Banno was an obedient disciple but he kept the copy and added some verses of Meera Bai and Surdas, which were initially rejected by the Guru. It is also alleged that he added some verses in the name of the first Guru. Guru Arjun Dev disapproved of this. This book is still said to be in the possession of Bhai Banno's descendants.

Coming Full Circle

History came full circle when Guru Gobind Singh declared the SGGS to be the next and only Guru after him. This marked the end of human guruship.

This did not happen easily. Guru Gobind Singh undertook the tedious task of preparing a new edition at Damdama Sahib or Talwandi Sabo. This new edition included all the hymns appearing in the original edition and the hymns of his late father Guru Tegh Bahadur. Guru Gobind Singh himself was a good poet but included only one of his hymns.

The task was completed in 1705. This edition is often called the *Damdama Sahib Bir*. It was installed on a high pedestal and given the status of '**Eternal Guru**'. The SGGS became the successor of the Guru in 1708. Bhai Nandlal, one of the disciples of Guru Gobind Singh, recorded the words of the Guru as given in the *Rohitnama*:

He who wishes to see the Guru,
Let him come to see the Granth,
He who wishes to speak to him,
Let him read and reflect upon what says the Granth,
He who wishes to hear his words,
He should with all his heart read the Granth.

There is a story of how this sacred *Granth* was once lost. The widow of Guru Gobind Singh, Mata Sundari, appointed Bhai Mani Singh as the *head granthi* of Harmandir Sahib. He was going to Amritsar with the volume of the sacred *Granth* in 1721, which was carried by the Sikhs ahead of marching troops. During the second Sikh Holocaust on February 5, 1762, the sacred volume was lost during battle. Fortunately, copies were made during the intervening years, so this tragic loss did not prove disastrous. This very text is the official and authorised version of *Sri Guru Granth Sahib*. A copy of the sacred scripture is there in every Gurudwara now.

SGGS is worshipped as the spirit, the infinite power and eternal energy of the one and only, the formless Supreme

Lord. Sikhs recite the verses and hymns and live up to their teachings.

Gurus' Verses

Guru Nanak was superior to all other saints of his time. He enjoyed royal dignity. In fact, he was a man free from worldly cares and anxieties and taught freedom to all.

The sacred scripture *Sri Guru Granth Sahib* enjoys the royal power and dignity of the Guru. Reading the holy scripture transforms the minds of people.

The Guru

Nanak is called *Guru* Nanak, which means he taught people and imparted knowledge. He is also called *Baba*, which means *grandfather* or *old master*. He always received respect usually accorded to grandparents. Guru Nanak is also called *Shah*, the shortened form of a Persian word *Badshah*. He was honoured like a Badshah during his lifetime.

SGGS is the representative of both the human *Guru* and the Absolute *Nirankari*. Whether Sikh or non-Sikh, all bow when facing it or prostrate and touch their forehead in reverence.

Guru Nanak was born with a mission in life. Prevalent religious rituals and traditions disillusioned him. Dissatisfied with prevalent social practices, the unseen forces of Nature and the cosmos moulded his mind and character, intelligence and perception, and helped him in fulfilling his mission.

As there is a definite reason behind the birth of Guru Nanak, so the SGGS came into being as a strong effect of it to awaken all sleeping human beings. As a true representative of the Guru and *Wahe Guru*, it silently completes its duty and achieves its spiritual goal.

The Divine Guru

Guru Nanak always talked of his divine Guru, who showed him the path, enlightened him and made him move on the chosen path to unite all. He had no human teacher. He had the vision of the formless Absolute. He made that vision his Guru, which was none other than the invisible Absolute Lord:

"The Guru of Gurus who is but one, the Hari."

And if the Guru is one, the pupils must be one. If the parent is one, the children must be one. If the emperor is one, the subjects must be one. So, a day after his revelation, he declared:

"There is no Hindu and no Muslim."

Themes of SGGS

The 'Oneness' is both the cause and the resultant effect in SGGS in which the *Sakhis*, *Vanis*, teachings and renderings of the Sikh Gurus, Hindu Saints and Muslim Sufis are amalgamated to declare that all religions are one for the Almighty is one, Mother Earth is one, Father Sky is one and the Creator is one. So, all human beings are ONE.

The other refrain of SGGS is '*purity*' – purity of the inner self and in the deeds. Impure, evils are never sanctioned by it. Crops grow as per the seeds we sow; likewise, if the seed is dead or impure it can never germinate. So one must abide by good moral conduct and imbibe every pure, humane characteristic.

Guru Nanak condemned blind adherence to tradition and did not accept idol worship. He had no faith in 'incarnations' of God, boldly renounced 'untouchability' but not the world or the home. First he himself practised everything, then taught others and asked them to follow what he thought to be the purest path. SGGS embodies all the pure and sublime.

Guru Nanak proclaimed moral values to be of supreme importance in everyday life. He believed in the formless *Nirgun* God. He preferred to lead a normal domestic and social life with a sense of equality and compassion. He did good and asked others to do good without expecting any reward. He was detached like the *Nishkam Karmayogi* of the Gita.

In a nutshell, SGGS says that nobody is high or low, Hindu or Muslim. The one and only God – who is truth, formless, infinite, unfathomable and indescribable – has created all. Each person should show the highest degree of humility, which can be achieved by universal brotherhood, equality and oneness. With the varied elements it contains, SGGS is capable of uniting all into one. SGGS shows the path and leads us all to a happy, pious and blissful life.

Remarkable Scripture

The *Adi Granth* or *Sri Guru Granth Sahib* is the eleventh and last Guru of the Sikhs who believe only in the Gurus and the *Adi Granth*.

The Sikh scripture SGGS is the greatest work of Punjabi literature that includes the *vani* of all prophets. It's *Guru Vani*, 'the loving voice of the Gurus'.

1.	**Guru Nanak**	**1469–1539**
2.	**Guru Angad**	**1504–1552**
3.	**Guru Amar Das**	**1479–1574**
4.	**Guru Ram Das**	**1534–1581**
5.	**Guru Arjun Dev**	**1563–1606**
6.	**Guru Har Gobind**	**1595–1644**
7.	**Guru Har Rai**	**1630–1661**
8.	**Guru Har Krishan**	**1656–1664**
9.	**Guru Tegh Bahadur**	**1621–1675**
10.	**Guru Gobind Singh**	**1666–1708**

A remarkable feature of the SGGS is that it includes the writings of other religious teachers of Hinduism and Islam.

1.	**Beni**	**12th Century**
2.	**Jaydeva**	**12th Century**
3.	**Baba Farid**	**12th Century**
4.	**Sadhna**	**13th Century**
5.	**Trilochana**	**13th Century**
6.	**Namdeva**	**13th Century**
7.	**Ramananda**	**14th Century**
8.	**Sain**	**14th Century**
9.	**Pipa**	**15th Century**
10.	**Kabir**	**15th Century**
11.	**Ramdas**	**15th Century**
12.	**Dhanna**	**16th Century**
13.	**Bhikham**	**16th Century**
14.	**Surdas**	**16th Century**
15.	**Parmananda**	**16th Century**

It is remarkable in another way also. It regards the word of Guru as the music that seers hear in their moments of ecstasy. The word of the Guru is considered to be the highest scripture.

Japji declares: *Gurumukhi nadam, gurumukhi vedam*; the voice from the Guru's mouth is the *Veda*, the *book of knowledge*. On the other hand, Guru Arjun Dev declared: *Pothi parmeswar ka dham*, the book is the *abode of God.*

In his article, *Adi Granth and the Sikh Religion*, Dr S. Radhakrishnan wrote: "The Sikh Gurus who compiled the *Adi Granth* had this noble quality of appreciation of whatever was valuable in other religious traditions. The saints belong to the whole world. They are universal men, who free our minds from bigotry and superstition, dogma and ritual and emphasise the central simplicities of religion. The great seers of the world are the guardians of inner values who correct the fanaticism of their superstitious followers. It is needless to state that the Sikh Gurus were all great seers of the world, for they transcend the opposition between the personal and the impersonal, between the transcendent and the immanent. The Gurus are the light-bearers to mankind. They are messengers of the timeless. They do not claim to teach a new doctrine but only to renew the eternal wisdom."

"The Guru is the in-dwelling divine who teaches all through the gentle voice of conscience. He appears outside in human form to those who crave for a visible guide. It is true because surrender to God becomes easy in the company of a saintly teacher, a Guru."

The reference to the Epilogue provided by Guru Arjun Dev becomes important and eloquent.

The words 'everybody' and 'everywhere' radiates with rich inner content because of the inclusion of songs and *sakhis* of other religions. It proves that the Guru and Sikhism were far above narrow considerations of caste, creed, cult and province. This is the real reason behind the immense success and amazing popularity of the SGGS which is a '*living and growing religion in itself*'. Its message of love and harmony is always listened to with rapt attention throughout the length and breadth of the subcontinent of India as well as surrounding lands. *It will remain immortal.*

Guru Vani
Excerpts from
Sri Guru Granth Sahib

गुरु वाणी

श्री गुरु ग्रन्थ साहिब
के
कथान

1. ੧ਓ

The Infinite, transcendental Lord, the Supreme God is the one whom Nanak has known as his Master.

Sorath, 559

2. ੧ਓ

There is but one True Lord in the whole world, there is no other. ***Dhansari, 660***

3. ੧ਓ

God is the only Spouse, all other beings are His brides.

Ramkali, 993

4. ੧ਓ

My master is one, one alone, one-in-one. ***Asa, 350***

5. ੧ਓ

I am a slave of the Supreme Lord and my name is 'Lucky'. I was sold at the Master's shop at *His* bidding and now I go the way *He* bids. ***Maru, 992***

6. ੧ਓ

God does everything and causes others to do whatever *He* wills. Nanak, the poet of the Lord, says that he also knows everything. ***Asa, 434***

7. ੧ਓ

The immaculate name of God alone is my sole base.

Asa, 412

8. ੧ਓ

Your fear, O God, is my hemp and my mind is the pouch which holds it; and I have thus become intoxicated with your love. ***Tilang, 721***

9. ੧ਓ

I spoke only when you, O God, inspired me to speak.

Wadhans, 566

10. ੧ਓ

I am the Lord's bard of low-caste. ***Asa, 468***

11. ੧ਓ

There is a dearth of truth, falsehood prevaileth; the blackness of this age maketh men demons. ***Dhansari 668***

12. ੧ਓ

As the world comes to me, so I make it known, O Lalo.

Tilang, 722

13. ੧ਓ

By repeating God's name, I live; by forgetting it, I die.

Asa, 9

14. ੧ਓ

The fire of anger is fatal. ***Sri, 15***

15. ੧ਓ

Any food, any dress, any mode of living is good provided that it promotes health of mind and body.

"Jit khade, jit paidhe, tan piriye man mahi chale vikar."

Sri Rag I

16. ੧ਓ

Our good and bad deeds shall be judged in the presence of the Supreme Judge. ***Jap, 8***

17. ੧ਓ

He indeed is mad who holds the master dear and considers himself unworthy and the rest of the world good. ***Maru, 991***

18. ੧੮

Thousands may endear you, thousands of lives you may live and enjoy in abundance the pleasures of life, separation from which seems poisonous while alive, yet when the parting comes, all these vanish in an instant.

Sarang, 1243

19. ੧੯

Practising austerities to subdue desires only wears off the body. The mind is not subdued through fasting, penances and self-torture. Nothing equals God's name. It helps in obtaining the desired state. ***Ramkali, 905***

20. ੨੦

God alone knows how great He is. ***Jap, 5***

21. ੨੧

Forgiveness for one who imbibes its spirit is as virtuous as fasting, good conduct and contentment. One who can forgive is neither afflicted by any ailment nor tortured by the regent of death. ***Gauri, 223***

22. ੨੨

When one passes out of life, all false ties are snapped.

Sri, 16

23. ੨੩

The blasphemer burns in his fire of hell. ***Majh, 132***

24. ੨੪

Wearing such clothes that cause pain and inconvenience to the body and breed evil in the mind is baneful, brother. ***Sri, 16***

25. ੧ੳ

There is but one God only. His name is Eternal Truth. He is the creator of the universe and the maker of everyone and everything. He is devoid of fear and enmity. He is immortal, unborn and self-existent: and is made known to men by the grace of the Guru, the Enlightener. ***Invocation, 1***

26. ੧ੳ

Millions have perished for want of compassion and forbearance. ***Ramkali, 937***

27. ੧ੳ

God alone kills the beings in His will and restores life to them if He so wishes. None else can sustain and protect them. ***Majh, 150***

28. ੧ੳ

Lack of compassion is like butchery. ***Sri, 91***

29. ੧ੳ

My breath, flesh and soul – all are yours, O Lord. To me you are extremely dear, O you the true provider of all, so says Nanak, the poet. ***Dhansari, 660***

30. ੧ੳ

I am a peddler of my all-pervading Lord and deal only in the merchandise of His Name. ***Gauri, 158***

31. ੧ੳ

With my hands as the begging-bowl, I crave nothing but your vision which I beg day after day at your door. Bless me Lord with your gracious sight. I call as a beggar at your gate. ***Tilang, 721***

32. ੧ੳ

God is just and does justice according to our deeds.

Sarang, 1238

33. ੧ੳ

The angry one barks, abuses and suffers humiliation in return. ***Malar, 1288***

34. ੧ੳ

God was true in the beginning. He was true throughout the ages. He is true even now and true forever He shall be. ***Jap, 14***

35. ੧ੳ

Calumny of others amounts to the impurity of ears.

Asa, 472

36. ੧ੳ

The craving of the fool is never satiated. ***Malar, 1287***

37. ੧ੳ

One's pain is one's own. ***Bilawal, 795***

38. ੧ੳ

While counting and fixing an auspicious day, we forget that God is above and beyond such considerations.

Ramkali, 904

39. ੧ੳ

All deeds and ceremonies performed in ego are nothing but entanglements. ***Asa, 416***

40. ੧ੳ

O, the inner-knower of all hearts, all living beings belong to you. ***Maru, 1038***

41. ੴ

God Himself is the relisher, Himself the relish, Himself the enjoyer and Himself the enjoyment. He Himself is the bride and Himself the spouse. He is my master who is deeply in love and pervades all. ***Sri, 23***

42. ੴ

Compassion is not awakened by beholding a supplicant's face. In the present age, none moves for another without the understanding of give and take. ***Asa, 350***

43. ੴ

I was a bard out of work. God blessed me with His service and commanded me to sing His praises night and day. He summoned me to His Eternal Abode, bestowed upon me the Robe of the Praise of His true Name and fed me with the Nectar-Name of the Great Truth. ***Majh, 150***

44. ੴ

After robbing a house if a thief offers the loot in worship to propitiate his ancestors, it will be recognised in the world beyond and thus impeach the departed souls as thieves. Justice bids the chopping off of the middleman's hands too, for we get hereafter what we give here out of our honest earnings. ***Asa, 472***

45. ੴ

God Himself is the Primal Truth, beauty and eternal bliss. ***Jap, 4***

46. ੴ

An angry disposition is ruinous. ***Sri, 91***

47. ੴ

All that we see is bound to come and go. ***Maru, 1021***

48. ੧ਓ

We are men of but one breath, and do not even know the span of our life and the time of our death.

Dhansari, 660

49. ੧ਓ

Avarice is a dog, falsehood the scavenger, and cheating is the eating of carrion. ***Sri, 15***

50. ੧ਓ

The generous give but a little in charity, but demand a thousand-fold return, with worldly honour to boot.

Asa, 466

51. ੧ਓ

Hunger befriends the taste and lust befriends beauty in the same way and to similar extent. ***Malar, 1208***

52. ੧ਓ

The ego degrades man from the human height and order.

Asa, 459

53. ੧ਓ

They who live with the Name of God are beyond the reach of death. ***Jap, 2***

54. ੧ਓ

Some call me a goblin, some a spirit. Some call me a mere forsaken man. But I, mad Nanak, have lost my reason in pursuit of the king, and I know none else but God. ***Maru, 991***

55. ੧ਓ

He who creates all, sustains them too. The creator who has made this world, fosters it too. ***Asa, 467***

Gurudwara Patal Puri (Punjab)

Gurudwara Rakab Ganj (New Delhi)

56. ੧ਓ

God pervades everywhere and drives all under His will.

Maru, 1042

57. ੧ਓ

Fear and love of God must co-exist in an earnest heart.

Asa di Var, 5.2

58. ੧ਓ

The true ablution consists in constant adoration of God.

Asa, 358

59. ੧ਓ

No bath can purify a body defiled by falsehood. Ablution is accepted only if one practices truth. *Wadhans, 566*

60. ੧ਓ

Birth and death are God's will and through His will men come and go. *Asa, 472*

61. ੧ਓ

Some seek heaven, others Paradise, but Nanak says that he who realises the Will and the Lord, knows the Mystery of the one, all powerful God. *Ramkali, 5*

62. ੧ਓ

O Creator, You belong to all, You are for all alike.

Asa, 360

63. ੧ਓ

Accursed is the life which is lived only to fill one's belly.

Suhi, 790

64. ੧ਓ

Avarice is the impurity of mind and falsehood the impurity of tongue. *Asa, 472*

65. ੧ਓ

Men come and go as God wishes and ordains. *Jap, 4*

66. ੧ਓ

Just shed off your ego and merge in God. *Subi, 750*

67. ੧ਓ

Wherever we sit or go we must behave and speak well.

Wadhans, 566

68. ੧ਓ

The glories of the great God can't be described. He is the Creator, the Supreme Almighty and the Beneficent One who provides sustenance to all living beings.

Asa, 475

69. ੧ਓ

However a saintly garb a man may wear, he can't conceal his inward impurity. *Gauri,*

70. ੧ਓ

There is but one benefactor of all creatures. *Jap, 2*

71. ੧ਓ

Everyone is answerable to God. No one is saved but for his good deeds. *Ramkali, 952*

72. ੧ਓ

The men of God have neither envy nor enmity.

Ramkali, 942

73. ੧ਓ

He changes many garbs and wanders to many places but there is deceit in his heart. He can't reach the palace of God. After death he will become a heath full of filth.

Majh

74. ੧ਓ

For shelter, safety and sustenance there is none but the One Lord to go to. *Asa, 475*

75. ੧ਓ

God is attained by loving and adoring the True Guru. *Sorath, 597*

76. ੧ਓ

You have neither worshipped God, nor fed the hungry, nor controlled lust, anger, greed and backbiting, O brother; what have you gained from reading *Puranas*. All your efforts have gone in vain. *Sarang*

77. ੧ਓ

How can You be angry with Your own children, O Lord, for You belong to them and they belong to You. *Sri, 25*

78. ੧ਓ

Whosoever tastes poison will die irrespective of his caste. Caste has no power. It is the righteousness that is tested. *Majh, 142*

79. ੧ਓ

When we see the same God within all, then whom can we call bad, and whom good. The Master has revealed the truth that all are alike. *Asa, 353*

80. ੧ਓ

Shape, beauty, possessions, caste and dominions are all deceivers. They have desired the whole world, and the honour of no one is safe from them. But they are also overcome by one who takes shelter in the True Master. *Malar, 1288*

81. ੧ੳ

None could have culture save through the word.

Malar, 1285

82. ੧ੳ

God's will runs over all and all merge in His will.

Basant, 1188

83. ੧ੳ

Men come and go in accordance with God's will.

Gauri, 151

84. ੧ੳ

He whose heart is corrupt and yet calls himself a saint is a hypocrite who can never realise God. *Sri*

85. ੧ੳ

Hereafter, man's words and deeds are scrutinised and he is brought to book for them. *Asa, 404*

86. ੧ੳ

Charity should be dispensed with wisdom. *Sarang, 1245*

87. ੧ੳ

From one flesh (cell) grows another flesh (cell). All our relationships are with the things of flesh (cell).

Malar, 1289

88. ੧ੳ

We are finally delivered if God Himself delivers us, for He alone can punish or forgive us. *Sri, 62*

89. ੧ੳ

He whose heart is polluted yet he shows himself to be pure has lost the game of life. *Ramkali*

90. ੧ਓ

All living beings belong to Him. ***Asa, 354***

91. ੧ਓ

Nanak says that those who are pure from inside live with the Guru forever. ***Ramkali***

92. ੧ਓ

All are yoked to God's will and will be judged according to their deeds. ***Basant, 1169***

93. ੧ਓ

A man's conduct can be true only if he cherishes the True One within his heart. ***Bilawal, 831***

94. ੧ਓ

They who know God here recognise Him hereafter too. The rest, Hindu or Muslim, is all a vain boast.

Ramkali, 952

95. ੧ਓ

All food is pure for God Himself has blessed us with it as sustenance. ***Asa, 472***

96. ੧ਓ

God is attained by His grace. All other ways that are boasted about are vain and false. ***Jap, 7***

97. ੧ਓ

He is towards the Guru (*Guru Mukh*) who is imbued with the Holy Name. ***Prabhati, 1330***

98. ੧ਓ

He, who calls himself a saint but his mind is full of deceit and desire, meets the end in shame. ***Gujri***

99. ੧੬

True is God, true is His court. We are judged there by our deeds. ***Jap, 7***

100. ੧੬

Know people by the light illuminating them and do not ask their caste as hereafter none is differentiated by one's caste. ***Asa, 349***

101. ੧੬

We are conceived of flesh, born of flesh and are the vessels of flesh. ***Malar, 1290***

102. ੧੬

God was true in the beginning. He was true throughout the ages. He is true even now and He shall ever be true. ***Jap, 1***

103. ੧੬

Those who are lost in greed and passion cannot cheat the Master. They may make show of their piety but are intoxicated with the worldly wine of Maya. They have to pass through many births and suffer according to their actions. ***Gauri***

104. ੧੬

He who gets God's grace attains Him, is freed from hope and greed, lust and fear, and burns down his ego with the help of the word. ***Asa, 468***

105. ੧੬

The pride of caste and the glory of name is nonsense, as each of us shelters under one and the same God.

Sri, 89

106. ੧ਓ

Man should remain detached realising that everything belongs to God. He should dedicate his body and mind to Him to whom they actually belong. ***Bilawal, 832***

107. ੧ਓ

Creation is the union of matter and spirit. In this creation I see the Creator pervading everywhere. ***Sri, 21***

108. ੧ਓ

Corn is heavenly, so are water, fire and salt. With the addition of clarified butter as the fifth, food becomes purer, holier and healthier. ***Asa, 473***

109. ੧ਓ

He who submits to His will is accepted and elevated by Him. ***Asa, 421***

110. ੧ਓ

God, the Guru, is attained by loving adoration.

Maru, 1042

111. ੧ਓ

If your heart is crooked what is the use of going on a pilgrimage to Kaaba or saying the *Namaz*. ***Prabhati***

112. ੧ਓ

Thieves, adulterers, prostitutes and pimps keep company together, just like the irreligious who eat and drink out of the same bowl. The Satan resides in them. They don't know the worth of God's praise. ***Subi, 790***

113. ੧ਓ

Truth is higher than anything else but truthful living is higher still. ***Sri, 62***

114. ੧ਓ

You are perfect, while we are imperfect. You are profound, while we are shallow, O God. *Sorath, 597*

115. ੧ਓ

Only the Lord is true and His name is true. *Jap, 2*

116. ੧ਓ

Call everyone high, none seems to be low, for God, the only Potter, has fashioned all alike, and His light alone pervades all creation. *Sri, 62*

117. ੧ਓ

Man should live and do as God wills. *Sri, 25*

118. ੧ਓ

Whatever happens, happens according to His will.

Gauri, 151

119. ੧ਓ

Falsehood and deceit can't remain concealed for long. It comes out and the false appearance vanishes.

Gauri

120. ੧ਓ

The leader or the teacher is himself deluded and misleads others, who indulge in falsehood and usurps what is not his, and yet goes to preach to others. *Majh, 140*

121. ੧ਓ

The Creator abides in the universe and keeps all creation in His eyes and feels delighted to see it. *Asa, 463*

122. ੧ਓ

The food that causes pain to body and breeds evil in mind is baneful. *Sri, 16*

123. ੧੬

The holy congregation is the meeting of good men in which only the Name of the One is sung and recited.

Sri, 72

124. ੧੬

O True God! The True King! Your plan and play are true.

Sri, 25

125. ੧੬

The truth is clear that God lives amongst all His people and is not to be found in stones. ***Tilang***

126. ੧੬

Beauty does not satiate one's craving for it. The more one sees it, the more one desires. ***Malar, 1288***

127. ੧੬

Live detached amidst attachments like the lotus in water.

Malar, 1281

128. ੧੬

Men get what they are destined for. ***Jap, 6***

129. ੧੬

The bond between Man and God is established only through His praise. ***Majh, 143***

130. ੧੬

Make your transient life your shop and the True Divine Name your only merchandise. Make alertness and purity your warehouse. Treasure the Name of God in it. Deal only with the Lord's dealers. You will get a fair profit and remain happy. ***Sorath, 595***

131. ੧ਓ

The Guru is the ladder, the boat, the raft in getting access to God's Name. ***Sri, 17***

132. ੧ਓ

He takes a bath and worships a stone; without the love of God he is full of dirt. ***Ramkali***

133. ੧ਓ

I eat whatever You give me, there is no door other than Yours to go. ***Sri, 25***

134. ੧ਓ

The will of one God alone pervades all the worlds, as all creation is born out of Him. ***Gauri, 223***

135. ੧ਓ

By nature, fools always talk something meaningless.

Majh, 143

136. ੧ਓ

You are the Master of Nature, its Creator Lord, your nature works everywhere. ***Asa, 464***

137. ੧ਓ

O brother! Domestic affairs are a whirlpool. ***Maru, 990***

138. ੧ਓ

If you do not think evil of others, my friend, no one will think evil of you. ***Asa, 134***

139. ੧ਓ

No one can equal Him. ***Sorath, 597***

140. ੧ਓ

Strike him on the face to mend a fool. ***Majh 143***

141. ੧੬

Brothers, do not think evil of others, then no evil will come to you. ***Gauri***

142. ੧੬

For the man of God, the Nada and Veda are reflection on the Word. His absolution and code of conduct are also based on it. ***Ramkali, 932***

143. ੧੬

God Himself is true and it is only truth that He likes. ***Sri, 25***

144. ੧੬

Those who are conscious of God are blessed with the name, compassion and purity. They are naturally attuned to God. ***Ramkali, 942***

145. ੧੬

The man of God speaks the truth and is never false. He follows the Guru's word and lives according to God's will. ***Gauri, 227***

146. ੧੬

The right way to live is to earn through toil and to share the earnings with others. ***Sarang, 1255***

147. ੧੬

The body is the palace, the temple, the house of God; in it He has put His infinite light. ***Malar, 1256***

148. ੧੬

An ignorant mind leads to ignorant action. Unless one follows the path shown by the Guru, he can't get rid of his ignorance. ***Basant, 1190***

149. ੧੪੯

God created Nature and He pervades it. *Sri, 84*

150. ੧੫੦

The idol neither feeds the hungry nor rescues the dying. *Sarang, 124*

151. ੧੫੧

God can neither be shaped nor installed like an idol. *Jap, 2*

152. ੧੫੨

O you, who live in Nature! I am a sacrifice unto You. *Asa, 469*

153. ੧੫੩

Those who are full of jealousy for others shall never get peace. *Gauri*

154. ੧੫੪

The Hindus are going the wrong way. They are drifting away from the Primal Lord. They worship stone idols. The ignorant fools don't realise that the stones themselves will sink in the sea of existence. It cannot ferry others across. *Bihag, 556*

155. ੧੫੫

I have found the whole world enveloped by mammon. *Asa, 354*

156. ੧੫੬

We should eat little, sleep little, but reflect a lot on the reality of life. *Ramkali, 939*

157. ੧੫੭

Metal melts into metal, love runs unto love. *Tilang, 725*

158. ੧ੳ

Turn your intelligence into fine paper. Make love your mighty pen and mind your conscious writer, then write the instructions given by the Guru. ***Sri, 16***

159. ੧ੳ

The sensuous man suffers from mental and physical diseases and undergoes great pain. ***Basant***

160. ੧ੳ

He Himself created Himself, assumed the Name. A second after Himself He created Nature, wherein He lives, pervades all and beholds all with delight. ***Asa, 463***

161. ੧ੳ

He who loves to see God does not care for salvation and paradise. ***Asa, 360***

162. ੧ੳ

The result of excessive indulgence is pain and misery. ***Basant, 1189***

163. ੧ੳ

Make compassion to be your mosque and faith your prayer-mat and honest living your Qur'an. Make modesty your circumcision and piety to be your fast. Only then you can be a true Muslim. ***Majh, 140***

164. ੧ੳ

Man claims to own everything but does not own the all pervading God who has created everything. ***Prabhati, 1343***

165. ੧ੳ

He who subdues his mind, subdues the world. ***Jap, 6***

166. ੧ੳ

Engrossed in lust, greed and pride, first man forgets God and then repents. ***Bihag***

167. ੧ੳ

Whoever comes to know God, becomes like Him.

Ramkali, 931

168. ੧ੳ

They who have silk within and rags outside are the really good ones of the world. ***Asa, 473***

169. ੧ੳ

Good are they who are adjudged good at God's Gate. Evil doers will sit outside and cry. ***Sri, 15***

170. ੧ੳ

Nothing can escape the attention of God who notices even a tiny insect that goes about picking grain, then how can he escape from His vision who indulges in everything that pleases him and assumes to be himself great. ***Asa, 360***

171. ੧ੳ

Like life, mind is born of the five elements. ***Asa, 415***

172. ੧ੳ

Water quenches one's thirst but it can't clean up one's dirty mind. ***Sarang, 1240***

173. ੧ੳ

Those who are false within and honourable in the eyes of others, who present a false face before the world, will never be able to wash their dirt away even if they bathe in sixty-eight holy rivers. ***Asa, 473***

174. ੧ਓ

They were honoured by God who kept death before their eyes and relied and equipped themselves with the Name of the Lord. ***Sri***

175. ੧ਓ

High and low come to be by His will. ***Jap, 1***

176. ੧ਓ

The impurity from touch is not impurity, but superstition. ***Asa, 472***

177. ੧ਓ

Desires direct a person and make his mind accordingly. ***Prabhati, 1342***

178. ੧ਓ

He alone is a Muslim who scrubs himself clean. ***Dhansari, 662***

179. ੧ਓ

He who recites and practises the Name of God is educated, learned and wise. ***Malar, 1288***

180. ੧ਓ

That alone is good who pleases God. ***Jap, 4***

181. ੧ਓ

Man becomes good in good company, pursues virtues and cleans himself of his vices. ***Asa, 414***

182. ੧ਓ

He who forgets God and indulges in sensuous pleasures suffers from all sorts of internal and external pain. ***Malar, 1256***

183. ੧ੳ

God's benediction amply descends there where the lowly are fostered with care. ***Sri, 15***

184. ੧ੳ

If God so wills He can keep man alive without breath. ***Gauri, 5***

185. ੧ੳ

By keeping our mind at peace in its own place, we come to know the mystery of both the visible and invisible world and phenomena. ***Sri, 57***

186. ੧ੳ

Only a few know and realise that mammon has lured the world and taken it over. ***Sorath, 595***

187. ੧ੳ

The world is led astray by paltry mammon. ***Ramkali, 932***

188. ੧ੳ

One loses the fear of birth and death in the love of God. ***Sri***

189. ੧ੳ

The company of those who cherish the True Lord within turns mortals into holy beings. ***Gauri, 228***

190. ੧ੳ

Do not call anyone bad and do not pick up a quarrel. ***Wadhans, 566***

191. ੧ੳ

An evil mind and indecision lead men to blind acts who grope about in the darkness waywardly. ***Basant, 1190***

192. ੧ਓ

Nanak seeks the company of the lowliest of the lowly, the lowest of the low born, for he knows that the emulation of the high born is in vain. ***Sri, 15***

193. ੧ਓ

One finds the mind of others as his own mind is.

Prabhati, 1342

194. ੧ਓ

Rituals and ceremonies are the chains of life. ***Sorath, 635***

195. ੧ਓ

As the rays of the Sun gather again in the Sun and the drop mingles with the Ocean, so does the light of man merge in God's light and he is fulfilled. ***Bilawal***

196. ੧ਓ

It's the most simple law, call no one bad. ***Asa, 473***

197. ੧ਓ

It is the purification that matters, for impurity is found in everything. Think of the worms, they have life in dung and rotten wood. ***Asa, 472***

198. ੧ਓ

Impurity of the mind is avarice. Impurity of the tongue is falsehood. Impurity of the eyes is to be greedy for another man's woman, wealth and beauty. Impurity of ears is to listen to the ill of others. Nanak says that these impurities lead the souls of men bound to the city of the regent of death. ***Asa, 472***

199. ੧ਓ

There is no high or low degree or caste before the Almighty.

Jap, 7

200. ੴ

They who forget God are low caste creatures, for without His Name mortals are outcast and a wretched lot.

Asa, 10

201. ੴ

The fire of desires which engulfs the whole world is the real impurity. It is spread all over the earth, the oceans and at other places. *Asa, 413*

202. ੴ

Creation is like the myriad waves rising from the sea and then merging again into the source. *Nat, 4*

203. ੴ

All are not good, all are not bad. *Suhi, 728*

204. ੴ

Good conduct, in accordance with the Guru's teaching, is in itself the praise of God. *Prabhati, 1343*

205. ੴ

If you are fond of playing the game of love, surrender completely and follow the path, hand in hand, without fear or hesitation. *Sloka, 1422*

206. ੴ

The innumerous pleasures of body give equal number of misery to men. *Malar, 1287*

207. ੴ

In childhood we were ignorant and blind. In youth we were lured away by sin. In the third stage we gathered riches and when old, regretfully left all behind.

Ramkali

208. ੧ਓ

God's light is contained in all orders of beings and all orders are contained in God's light. *Asa, 419*

209. ੧ਓ

Out of Brahma, Vishnu, Shiva and Indra, out of all the seers, sages, saints, ascetics and mendicants, whoever obeys His command, is honoured by Him. But they who disobey Him, are surely destroyed by Him. *Maru, 992*

210. ੧ਓ

They who do not love, they do not taste the love of the Beloved. They are like guests who visit an empty house and return in utter disappointment. *Suhi, 790*

211. ੧ਓ

There is light among all which is the light of the Lord's own self. It pervades and enlightens everyone.

Dhansari, 663

212. ੧ਓ

Neither childhood nor youth nor age is safe from the clutches of death. Man is but a mouse, and the cat of death devours it to bring the end. *Bilawal*

213. ੧ਓ

Those stone-gods who are washed by water and sink into water cannot take one across the sea of turbulent existence.

Sorath, 636

214. ੧ਓ

Where there is good conduct, the understanding is perfect and life is pleasant. Without good conduct it is loss and loss only. *Sri, 25*

215. ੴ

Everyone craves for happiness, no one bears the misery.

Sri, 57

216. ੴ

The mortal indulges in vice and sin by drinking insipid worldly wine. *Bihag, 553*

217. ੴ

Tender and sweet speech increases, fosters and tightens the bond of love. *Majh, 13*

218. ੴ

O friend! Wealth does not keep company after death.

Sorath, 595

219. ੴ

One loads the boat of life with sin and launches it upon the sea, and lo, one sees not the yonder shore, nor the port to sail. The sea is dreadful and there is no boatman, nor the rows to row the boat across. *Maru*

220. ੴ

There is no limit to God's works and no end to His gifts.

Jap, 5

221. ੴ

Although one may run about a great deal but without good deeds nothing can be obtained. *Tilang, 722*

222. ੴ

One may read throughout one's life, read even with every breath, yet of all things, it is only the contemplative life that really matters. All else is the fret and prattle of ego.

Asa, 467

223. ੧ਓ

The Divine Light that dwells in the human mind, the human mind is its emanation. ***Ramkali, 878***

224. ੧ਓ

There is all and only outward love in this world. Every person thinks of his own gain though he may be a close kith or kin. ***Devgandhari***

225. ੧ਓ

All joys and sorrows come from God. ***Asa, 418***

226. ੧ਓ

He whose heart is in love attains salvation. ***Majh***

227. ੧ਓ

Pain and pleasure are part of God's will. ***Gauri, 223***

228. ੧ਓ

As all other deeds are fruitless, so dwell on only God's Name. ***Suhi, 728***

229. ੧ਓ

The sorrows of men are many like the numerous pleasures of the body. ***Malar, 1287***

230. ੧ਓ

He who takes the divine rector of Truth, does not relish insipid and unhealthy worldly wine. ***Asa, 360***

231. ੧ਓ

Man without love is an empty, dry shell which crumbles and is reduced to dust. ***Sri, 62***

232. ੧ਓ

He is true and His works are true. ***Jap, 7***

233. ੧ੳ

As one acts, so one is rewarded. ***Dhansari, 662***

234. ੧ੳ

A *Vaishnava* is he who knows no other but the Lord, and by the Guru's Grace, realises himself. ***Sri***

235. ੧ੳ

Man comes and goes by God's Will. His will dominates everywhere and everything, heretofore and hereafter.

Gauri, 151

236. ੧ੳ

Make your faith the soil, and truth the seed, then cultivate yourself. ***Asa, 418***

237. ੧ੳ

This body is the soil, our actions are the seed, we can irrigate it with the name of the Lord who holds the whole earth. ***Sri, 23***

238. ੧ੳ

One is approved and accepted only if one fully submits oneself to the will of the Lord. In His court only truth is accepted. ***Maru, 5090***

239. ੧ੳ

All abide in Thy Hope; on all hearts rains Thy Mercy. All are shareholders in Thy Grace; O dear Lord, Thou art alien to none. ***Majh***

240. ੧ੳ

An egotist is not true to his being (salt) and does not feel indebted to anyone for the good done to him.

Majh, 143

241. ੧ਓ

God does whatever He wills to do. ***Asa, 475***

242. ੧ਓ

Without the Guru all is darkness, and without the word we do not realise it. ***Sri, 55***

243. ੧ਓ

God's word is the Guru and the mind attuned to it is the disciple. ***Ramkali, 943***

244. ੧ਓ

A Muslim dwells on the Prophet's way but without wisdom. How can he know the end? Let thy bowing be of faith and knowledge of mind thy subject of study. ***Sloka, 1***

245. ੧ਓ

Knowledge is a cause of worry. The more we read and write, the more we worry. ***Asa, 467***

246. ੧ਓ

Knowledge cannot be sought through mere talk.

Malar, 1287

247. ੧ਓ

Thou art here, Thou art hereafter, all creatures are Thy own creation. ***Majh***

248. ੧ਓ

There is no other that does except Him. Whatever He willed has come to pass. ***Gauri, 154***

249. ੧ਓ

He alone knows the way who meets and obeys the Guru. Blessed with his word by the Guru he realises the will of the Lord. ***Ramkali, 984***

250. ੧ੳ

Let the mind be the ploughman, good deeds the ploughing, honest strivings the water and your body the field. Let God's name be the seed, contentment the leveller and humility the fence. By doing deeds of love, the seed will sprout. Blessed will be then your home. ***Sorath, 595***

251. ੧ੳ

Only that *pandit* is learned and well read who reflects on knowledge with cool calmness. ***Ramkali, 937***

252. ੧ੳ

Through wisdom we understand what we read and realise the true meaning. ***Sarang, 1245***

253. ੧ੳ

He understands the essence of the *Vedas*, *Puranas* and the *Smritis* and finds the apparent in the subtle. He instructs all the four castes in the Lord's wisdom. Nanak says that he salutes such a *pandit* forever. ***Gauri***

254. ੧ੳ

That alone happens which pleases God. Man is completely helpless. There is nothing in his hands and control.

Asa, 417

255. ੧ੳ

He who moves at the will of God never faces hindrances.

Asa, 421

256. ੧ੳ

He who forsakes the Lord's name and treads another path, falls into hell. He is punished in a myriad ways, crude and subtle, and he wanders from womb to womb.

Sarang, 5

257. ੴ

The name of God abides within the body. He himself is the creator and immortal and resides in us. ***Maru, 1026***

258. ੴ

That man does not go to hell who dwells on God's Name. ***Asa, 456***

259. ੴ

Ill-gotten food does not become lawful by seasoning it with sauce and spices. ***Majh, 141***

260. ੴ

Association with evil-doers is like poison which kills, they are destroyed and their life goes in vain. ***Prabhati, 1343***

261. ੴ

The knower of the Essence, He is beauteous and wise. He looks on all alike and sees the One in all. ***Gauri, 5***

262. ੴ

Liberation from bondage is effected by the will of God. Nothing else has a say in it. ***Jap, 5***

263. ੴ

None can go to heaven by talk alone. Salvation comes by being true and by living the Truth. ***Majh, 141***

264. ੴ

Burn the body which has forsaken the name of God. ***Suhi, 789***

265. ੴ

He alone is learned who does good to others. ***Asa, 356***

266. ੧ਓ

If the mind is impure, the body and the tongue also become impure. *Sri, 45*

267. ੧ਓ

Since we are not to live forever in the world, so never be angry with anyone. Simply drink the nectar of His name. *Ramkali, 931*

268. ੧ਓ

Heaven is not attained or obtained without good deeds. *Ramkali, 952*

269. ੧ਓ

She is the happiest wife who is dear to her husband. *Tilang, 722*

270. ੧ਓ

The body is bound down by the three dispositions. Whoever is born, he lives within these limits. *Sri, 21*

271. ੧ਓ

The body is not cleaned without the loving adoration of God. *Sri, 59*

272. ੧ਓ

He is beyond the reach of the regent of death who enjoys the protection of the Lord. *Malar, 1284*

273. ੧ਓ

The greatest wonder about God is that there is none other like Him, there never was, nor ever will be. *Asa, 349*

274. ੧ਓ

She is the happiest wife who has God as her spouse. *Sri, 56*

275. ੧ਓ

With the appearance of the sun, the moon disappears; with the attainment of knowledge, ignorance also disappears.

Suhi, 791

276. ੧ਓ

Let the continence be the forge, patience the goldsmith, understanding the anvil and knowledge the hammer. Let God's fear be the bellows, austerity the fire and God's love the crucible to melt the metal of life's nectar therein.

In this way the gold of life can be shaped, the divine word can be fashioned in that mint of truth for the everlasting bliss. But remember, only those who are blessed with God's grace can work at their lives in this way and only they can get the eternal bliss. ***Jap, 8***

277. ੧ਓ

The pitcher holds water yet it needs water to get its shape. So is the mind which holds the knowledge but without knowledge the mind cannot grow and get its shape, and knowledge too needs a mind without which it cannot get its existence and grow. The mind illumined by the Guru holds knowledge in greater quantity and of better quality.

Asa, 469

278. ੧ਓ

Religion does not consist in sitting at the tomb or in a burning ghat and diving deep in meditative pseudo-trance. It is neither in roaming here and there in the world nor taking holy bath at the places of worship. The way to true religion is found by remaining detached in the midst of worldly attachments. ***Suhi, 730***

279. ੧ੳ

What else can I say now but this, that where the saints are, that indeed, is heaven. *Kabir*

280. ੧ੳ

God is the only protection, nothing else. *Asa, 439*

281. ੧ੳ

There is one way, one love, one beauty that shines through air, water and fire, one bumble bee that roams the whole universe. He who understands this unity will be honoured. But few God-oriented realise it. They use their knowledge and meditation for such equipoise. He who gets it through his grace is happy. The way is shown to him through the Guru. *Ramkali Dakhni, 7*

282. ੧ੳ

Those who have ruined their crop in the field, their misdeeds cannot expect to gather grain and fill up their granary. *Sarang, 1245*

283. ੧ੳ

Lust summons and examines men and pronounces judgement on greed and sin. *Tilang, 627*

284. ੧ੳ

Whoever honestly cries and truly begs at the door of the Lord is duly heard, rewarded and blessed. *Asa, 349*

285. ੧ੳ

Priceless is He, our Lord, the God. Forsaking Him one is cast into hell where there is neither mother nor father, neither husband nor wife, neither friend nor kinsman to save him. *Maru, 5*

286. ੧ੳੰ

As by lighting the lamp, darkness is dispelled, so by reading religious books, the mind is cleaned of sins. ***Suhi, 791***

287. ੧ੳੰ

As one sows, so does one eat, as one acts, so is one rewarded.

Dhansari, 662

288. ੧ੳੰ

Whatever one sows, one reaps, whatever one earns, one eats. ***Suhi, 730***

289. ੧ੳੰ

He who indulges in greed, avarice and falsehood, reaps only what he sows. ***Sloka, 1411***

290. ੧ੳੰ

Those who serve One have perfect wisdom. His servants take shelter with the Pure One, who is from the beginning before the aeons began. O brother, there is none else, my Lord is one. Faith in Him, the True One, has brought joy to me through His grace. ***Asa, 3***

291. ੧ੳੰ

God can never be attained by any clever devices; we can attain him only by effacing ourselves. ***Tilang, 722***

292. ੧ੳੰ

Mere talk will not make us religious. He is truly religious who looks on all as alike and considers all as equal.

Suhi, 730

293. ੧ੳੰ

Bear, O my soul! The result of thine own acts.

Sloka, 9

294. ੧ੳ

God is one and has ever been the same, so he who grasps the truth easily realises that there is but only one religion for all mankind. ***Basant, 1188***

295. ੧ੳ

Everyone must bear the result of his own acts and adjust his own account. ***Gauri, 19***

296. ੧ੳ

Good works I have accepted as my spouse. ***Gauri***

297. ੧ੳ

I am that. That is I. ***Maru***

298. ੧ੳ

It is prayer, not the command, that pleases the Master.

Asa, 474

299. ੧ੳ

Wealth is accumulated with labour and pain and when it goes, it leaves us in deep pain. Only he is satiated who drinks sublime nectar of the Name of the Lord.

Malar, 1287

300. ੧ੳ

One Maya in union with God gave birth to three acceptable children. One of them the Creator, the second the Provider and the third the Destroyer. ***Japji, 30***

301. ੧ੳ

As saffron, flowers, musk and gold embellish the body and also does the scented sandal of the saints. They make all fragrant who come in contact with them. So, O Lord, I beg at Your door, bless me with Thy Grace. ***Sorath***

302. ੧ੴ

On the earth and in heaven, and in men and women of all the worlds, I see none other. In the shining lamps of the sun and the moon, I uninterrupted see my beloved, ever young. ***Gauri, 9***

303. ੧ੴ

Duality in the minds of creatures is an illusion, by which they are led to destruction through lust, anger and pride. ***Gauri, 9***

304. ੧ੴ

The whole visible creation is the body. Whatever we hear are Thy voice. Thou Thyself pervade all and art the enjoyer. ***Asa, 3***

305. ੧ੴ

No one is emancipated without the Lord's name, and dying one falls into hell. ***Asa, 1***

306. ੧ੴ

The Brahmins, the Kshatriyas, the Vaishyas and the Shudras are all emancipated if and when they contemplate on the Lord. ***Gauri, 5***

307. ੧ੴ

Caste or no caste one is saved singing, hearing and contemplating Him. O Mind, always praise the Lord. I know this way for I'm merged into my Creator Lord. ***Devgandhari, 5***

308. ੧ੴ

The buffalo is intoxicated with ego and is never disciplined. He tries to overwhelm others and is thrown into hell. ***Sloka, 5***

309. ੧ਓ

Through Him, the One, has sprung the whole creation. Men walk on two paths of good and evil but know that the Lord is One. Know His will through the Guru's word.

Gauri, 9

310. ੧ਓ

He who slanders the All-perfect and True Guru is destroyed by the Creator Lord. Opportunities do not come to him again. He eats what he sows. He is thrown into the depths of hell. His face is blackened and he is driven like a thief.

Sloka, 4

311. ੧ਓ

My Lord is One, O brother He is One. He Himself destroys and preserves. He Himself gives life and takes it back. He Himself looks after us and makes us bloom. He Himself showers His grace. What He wills He does, nothing can be done against His will. ***Asa, 3***

312. ੧ਓ

Wisdom that is imparted to all the four castes alike is the real wisdom. He who dwells on the Name of the All-pervading Lord is emancipated in the *kaliyuga*.

Suhi

313. ੧ਓ

Thou art the River of Wisdom and I a mere fish. How can I know Your infinite expansion? I see neither the net nor the fisherman but when in pain I call Thee. ***Sri***

314. ੧ਓ

Some offer Thee oblations, others bow down before Thee. But he who realises Thy will knows the mystery of the All-powerful God. ***Ramkali***

Gurudwara Parivar Vichhora Sahib

Govindwal Sahib (Punjab)

315. ੧ੳ

The kings are butchers and cruelty is their knife. The sense of responsibility and duty has taken wings and flown. ***Majh, 16***

316. ੧ੳ

Those who are sometimes good and sometimes bad are attacked by afflictions of the mind, body and soul. Their pain never leaves them. They never realise the glory of their All-perfect Transcendent Lord. So, they are drowned in the sea of doubt and attachment. They abide deep in hell. ***Gauri, 5***

317. ੧ੳ

The women who wore beautiful tresses have their locks shorn with scissors and dust is thrown upon their heads who have been dishonoured and are carried away by soldiers with ropes around their neck. ***Asa, 1***

318. ੧ੳ

Babur rushed down from Kabul with a big bridal procession of sin and forcibly demanded the hand of the bride India. People sing of the pangs of murder and smear themselves with saffron of blood. ***Tilang, 1***

319. ੧ੳ

The dogs have thrown away the invaluable gem; when they are dead and gone, no one will remember them with regard. ***Asa, 39***

320. ੧ੳ

He is deathless, unborn, casteless and without entanglements. He is unfathomable and beyond the reach of senses, without form or line. Searching and searching I found Him in every soul. ***Bilawal, 1***

321. ੧ੳ

The Lord is near, do not think He is distant. The One pervades the whole creation. Nanak is merged in Him for he knows one God and shuns duality. ***Gauri***

322. ੧ੳ

Be not proud of your caste for he alone is a Brahmin who knows Brahma, like only God. ***Bhairo***

323. ੧ੳ

The Lord loves His devotees. When He bestows His Grace, He comes to reside in our hearts. ***Sri***

324. ੧ੳ

Controlling the mind I became aware of the impurity-free state and got absorbed in the love of God more and more. Outside the One I recognise none. ***Sarang, 7***

325. ੧ੳ

In the eternal hour of fragrant dawn, think upon and glorify His name and greatness. ***Jap, 4***

326. ੧ੳ

Guided by the light of the Guru, the disciple steers himself safe and saves many other lives. ***Jap, 15***

327. ੧ੳ

He who sings the praise of the Lord for an instant, mounts to all the heaven and is released, freed and delivered.

Ashtpadi, 5

328. ੧ੳ

The Lord is near, far and in the middle, seeing, hearing and creating all by Himself. ***Sri***

329. ੧ਓ

He Himself corrects others. *Sri*

330. ੧ਓ

The sun moves during the day, the moon during the night, and millions of stars run in their courses. Nanak proclaims the truth that the one God alone remains unmoved.

Sri, 8

331. ੧ਓ

He was my support in the beginning and He is my support at the end. *Sri*

332. ੧ਓ

I feel lost in Him. All doubts and delusions have departed and the light shines within. *Ramkali, 931*

333. ੧ਓ

There is no other door to which I may go, so, this is the humble prayer of Thy servant Nanak: Accept my mind and body, O Lord, as fully devoted to Thee. *Sri, 25*

334. ੧ਓ

He is brave who possesses the strength but displays it not and lives in humble ways. *Majh*

335. ੧ਓ

Nanak says that his God is above and beyond the *Vedas* and Semantic texts. The process of coming, living and going is He, my Lord. *Asa*

336. ੧ਓ

He is the only shelter of the shelterless. He is the treasure of good, the everfresh being. His gifts are perfect.

Sri

337. ੴ

God can't be pleased with deceit and falsehood. ***Sri***

338. ੴ

Thy praisers praise Thee, and know not Thy greatness, as rivers and streams flow into the sea, but know not its vastness. ***Jap, 23***

339. ੴ

One may have riches, glory and piety in life; parents, children, friends and brothers; the army may salute him but if he does not remember the Lord in his heart, he suffers in the depths of hell and his life is meaningless.

Sri, 5

340. ੴ

When the body is dirty it is rinsed with soap, when the mind is polluted with sin it is scrubbed with the Name.

Jap, 20

341. ੴ

He who sees the same light pervade all forever and perceives the essence of the Guru's way, realizes the God in himself.

Sri

342. ੴ

The spouse favours the bride he likes and she is his only bride whom He honours by His grace. ***Sri***

343. ੴ

Let my tongue become a hundred thousand tongues and multiply twenty times. With each tongue I would repeat Thy holy name many hundred thousand times to allow the soul to ascend the stairs to go up to the bridegroom and be one with Him. ***Jap, 32***

344. ੧੬

I may have a pen filled with inexhaustible ink and write Thy praise with the speed of the wind, yet, I could not express Thy praise nor the greatness of Thy Name.

Sri, 14

345. ੧੬

He who is lost in the greed for worldly things is neither honoured here nor in another life. *Basant*

346. ੧੬

When we realise God in our inner selves, He blesses us with His grace and washes off our dirt. *Sri*

347. ੧੬

My master is all and sportive. He is the fish and the fisherman. He is the net and the river. *Sri*

348. ੧੬

God's grace is upon all but He gives to him whom He pleases. *Sri*

349. ੧੬

Thou sayest prayers five times, giving them five different names. Let truth be thy first prayer and honest living the second, and the good of all thy third prayer. Let the honest mind be the fourth prayer and the praise of the Lord, the fifth. That way thou pray the prayers of deeds and thus be thou a true Muslim. All other prayers are false and without value. *Majh, M 1*

350. ੧੬

He who dwells in and out on the Lord's name, who receives and follows instructions from the perfect Guru, and who abides with the holy, is naturally saved from hell.

Gauri, 5

351. ੧ੳ

Wherefrom the Hindus come? Wherefrom the Muslims? Who has created their different paths? O man of evil intent, reflect on it in your mind. Tell me, who is the creator of heaven and hell? O Kazi, which is the book that you have read, for they who read, reflect and react like you, are wasted away. They do not know the essence. ***Asa, Kabir***

352. ੧ੳ

First let the faith in Allah seem sweet to him and then let him scrub off his inside clean of ego. Then with faith he can break the illusion of life and death. When he submits to the will of Allah and believes in the Eternal Creator, only then he would lose his self or ego. Nanak says that if he is compassionate and kind to all creatures then he is taken as a true Muslim. ***Majh, M 1***

353. ੧ੳ

God alone does give and His giving has no bounds.

Asa

354. ੧ੳ

The Hindu is blind, the Muslim is one-eyed and the all-seeing wise is the one wise in God. Hindus worship at temples, Muslims at mosques but Namdeva worships the God, who has no temple and no mosque to call His own. ***Bilawal, Namdeva***

355. ੧ੳ

For many births we passed through the species of creeping insects and feathered worms, large elephants, swimming fish and running antelopes, remained yoked as horses and oxen. Now the Lord of the Universe after aeons of long time has given the human body. ***Gauri Guareri M 5***

356. ੧ਓ

Nanak says that he is the bravest among the brave who has overcome his inner ego. *Slokas*

357. ੧ਓ

When I meet my carefree Master I renounce my formative will and the noise of reason. *Sri*

358. ੧ਓ

If one enshrines the Lord in the mind he is emancipated, and looking godwards he merges in the Lord's truth. *Maru*

359. ੧ਓ

Everywhere is the God's seat and He has everywhere His stall and He puts in it all that He wills. *Jap, 31*

360. ੧ਓ

Thou art the honour and glory and Thou art the giver of them. *Sri*

361. ੧ਓ

Nanak says: Chop off the head that bows not to the Lord. The being not charged with love for Him is worthy only of being burnt. *Sri*

362. ੧ਓ

The Lord showers gifts on all. Though awake yet some receive not, and He blesses some by awakening them from sleep. *Sri*

363. ੧ਓ

He is emancipated and he is the released one who is affected neither by joy nor sorrow and looks upon friend and foe as one. *Sloka*

364. ੧ੳ

God is the enticing fortress of gold. He is a beauteous temple studded with jewels, rubies, pearls and diamonds.

Sri

365. ੧ੳ

By contemplating with the inner attention on the Supreme Word, the torrent of Divine Love has rushed down to the mind. The aspirant has merged in the Divine Lord and drinks the Nectar, the Celestial Drink, undrinkable to the mortals.

Kabir, 93

366. ੧ੳ

He who can be as high as He is, to that height He alone knows.

Jap, 24

367. ੧ੳ

The wise do not crave for emancipation nor entertain thoughts of heaven.

Maru

368. ੧ੳ

O Destroyer of pride, Thy share has faith only in Thee.

Sorath

369. ੧ੳ

They have received honour, they are exalted on the throne, in whose mind abides the Fearless One, and who have contemplated on Him; they have encompassed in their meditation, the solar systems, the continents, the countries, the lower regions, and all the three parts of the universe.

Maru Solhas, 1023

370. ੧ੳ

The frying pan of the mind has cooled down with the elixir of the Name given by the Guru.

Maru

371. ੧ਓ

The same Supreme Brahma I have seen with my eyes about whom it is written in the *Vedas* that it is the gracious habit of the Lord to purify the fallen. ***Bilawal, 805***

372. ੧ਓ

After being tired of searching the Lord by roaming about from forest to forest, then at last Nanak met the saints and found Hari in his own mind. ***Asa, 5th Guru, Sloka***

373. ੧ਓ

The path is clear of one who believes, lives with honour and with Grace he leaves. ***Jap***

374. ੧ਓ

Why wander you out and about in the wilderness, when thy God abides within thee. ***Gauri, 5***

375. ੧ਓ

God is the philosopher's stone that transmutes our iron into gold. He is the *chandan* tree that makes our dry wood fragrant. ***Dhansari, 4***

376. ੧ਓ

Nanak says that by the Grace of the Guru my doubts and errors are gone. He and I met and have become one.

Asa, M 5

377. ੧ਓ

The Lord is the cause of causes. There is not another without Him. ***Dhansari, 9***

378. ੧ਓ

My God is riches to the poor, staff to the blind and milk to the child. ***Dhansari, 5***

379. ੧ਓ

Wherever saints sit, at their feet the place is holy, and wherever the name of the Lord is uttered, that place is a paradise. ***Ramkali, 5***

380. ੧ਓ

Without experiencing the Bliss of Divine Love, the tongue chattered much ceaselessly and always nonsense. But after being empowered with the Bliss of Love, it has taken the vow of silence. It has sunk in the intoxication of love after drinking the divine drink called nectar. Now the attention is turned towards Him. ***Kabir, 81***

381. ੧ਓ

I do not blame others, I blame my own acts. As I acted so have I been rewarded. ***Asa, 433***

382. ੧ਓ

The Yogi, our Lord, the Supreme God, abides in the seedless state, who can neither be identified with man nor woman. ***Dhansari***

383. ੧ਓ

Make your Ramzan the fast of noble conduct. Thus you shall be a true Muslim. Make good deeds your Kaaba; truthfulness your preceptor, turn your *Nanak* and *Kalma* into pure action, with rosary will you please God. ***Bilawal***

384. ੧ਓ

Where egoism exists, Thou are not experienced, where Thou art is not egoism.
You who are learned, expound in your mind, this inexpressible preposition. ***Maru ki Var***

385. ੧ੳ

Have firm faith and let your mind not be shaken.

Dhansari

386. ੧ੳ

Forgive my past sins and show me the path now; killing my ego, I should remain in God's service.

Guru Amar Das

387. ੧ੳ

Saith Nanak, the saints hunger to praise Thee, the true name is their support. In everlasting joy they abide day and night, may I obtain the dust of the feet of such virtuous men?

Sloka, 6

388. ੧ੳ

Why do you go to the forest in search of God? He lives in all and is yet ever distinct. He abides with you, too, as fragrance dwells in a flower, and reflection in a mirror, so does God dwell inside everything. Seek Him, therefore, in your heart.

Jap

389. ੧ੳ

Those who believe in Him
Get to the gate of salvation
Those who believe in Him are
Saved with their kin
Those who believe in Him
Swim across and help others swim
Those who believe in Him
Don't have to beg of others
Such is the name of God, the Pure
Those who believe in Him
They alone get to know Him

Jap

390. ੧ਓ

Compassion and forgiveness should be your attainments.

Guru Gobind Singh

391. ੧ਓ

Permanence belongs to Him who no one controls. The heavens and earth will pass but the One God will remain unchanged.

Sri Rag, 8.17

392. ੧ਓ

Kings are like leopards and their revenue collectors dogs, they go and awaken people at all odd times. Their servants wound the people with their claws and lick their blood like curds.

Mahar, 22

393. ੧ਓ

If a powerful person were to attack another powerful person there shall be no grievance but if a ferocious lion were to fall upon a herd of cattle, the master of the herd has to answer for it.

Asa 1, 39-42

394. ੧ਓ

Myriads are yet asleep;
Deluded by the false mirage of Mammon;
They alone, O Nanak, are awakened;
Who repeat the Name Supreme by tongue.

Malar, 1425

395. ੧ਓ

Of whatever sort, He bestoweth
His Grace on any one,
Of that sort indeed, doth one become.
Without the gift of grace,
O Nanak, there is none.

Dhansari, 661

396. ੧ਓ

Those forgetting the Lord are the truly low-caste, Nanak saith. The fallen are those who live without God.

Suhi

397. ੧ਓ

The One alone existeth, yet, there is no other,
That One art Thou, O, that One art Thou.

Majh, 143

398. ੧ਓ

Without *vairagya*, Maya can't be got rid of. ***Sri, 329***

399. ੧ਓ

Whosoever I see, I see Thee pervading there;
There is no other such place where Thou art not.

Dhansari, 661

400. ੧ਓ

Exhausted after all effort, to the Lord's shelter I go,
Now that to His shelter I have come, say I,
"Lord, preserve me or ruin me as may please Thee."

401. ੧ਓ

The true Guru has made the One, Unfathomable and Unknowable by senses, clear to me. ***Sarang, 7.2***

402. ੧ਓ

He is the Mastermind and Birthless. Filled to the brim by His love my mind does not wander. Through itself it has found its stay. ***Sarang, 7.5***

403. ੧ਓ

Through the Guru I have realised the One, impurity free. Through the Word duality is destroyed. His decree rules all the world. ***Gauri, 9.5***

404. ੧ਓ

God is unknowable, unfathomable, all powerful, creator and compassionate. The whole world comes and goes but the merciful stays forever. ***Sri Rag, 8.17***

405. ੧ਓ

By this Grace, you enjoy all sorts of pleasures, you are provided with all the necessities of life and yet, you forsake Him and attach yourself to others, such sinful mistakes cling to fools.

406. ੧ਓ

By Omkar was created Brahma;
Who forever on Omkar meditates;
By Omkar were created the mountains and the aeons;
By Omkar were created the *Vedas*.
Meditation on Omkar brings emancipation;
By Omkar are the faithful saved;
Contemplate, O man, the exposition of the syllable Om;
In the syllable Om are epitomised the three worlds.

Bilawal

OO

The Eleven Gurus

I. Guru Nanak

It's one thing to follow a tradition, and quite a different proposition to create and become a tradition. Surprisingly enough, the Guru of the Sikhs followed not one but many traditions but created one *Omkar*; he began a new tradition of amalgamation, synthesis and purification. He was the real master and true teacher. Guru Nanak, the first Guru of the Sikhs and undoubtedly a rishi in India's glowing traditions of rishis, ruled and still rules over the hearts, minds and lives of millions.

Guru Nanak claimed: "The man who earns his bread by the sweat of his brow and gives some of his gains in charity knows the true way of life."

"Kar se kam karo, Hari se dhyan dharo," said Sant Kabir. (Work with your hands and keep your thoughts on God.)

The tradition of the *Brihadaranyaka Upanishad*, which reiterates that having created the ruler, to control him the Supreme Being created *dharma*, was accepted and depicted by Guru Nanak:

Man set in authority!
Let devotion be thy service,
Let thy toil be faith in the Name,
Check thy mind from wandering after temptation.
Stand on guard against all evil,
So from all men thou shalt earn the praise
And the Lord, thy King,
Will delight in thee
With a fourfold increase in His love.

Guru Nanak did not conduct his mission in isolation or wholly in passive meditation or holy exercises in retirement. He took a leading, active and decisive part in public and political affairs, in personal and social life, in individual and collective religion.

Guru Nanak draws his strength from the inexhaustible depths of one's self and contemplation, introspection and prayer, for all such introspection and prayer can help find *Nivriti* in *Pravriti* and *Pravriti* in *Nivriti* in keeping with the *Karma Yoga* taught by the *Gita*. This *Karma Yoga* is the core of Guru Nanak's thought and *Vani*. It is the root that gives sap and strength to the great, growing, green tree of Sikhism.

II. Guru Angad

Guru Angad is Bhai Lehna, who was born at village Harike in Ferozepur district, Punjab on March 31, 1504. He was the son of a trader **Pheruji** and **Mata Ramoji**. His grandfather lived at Matte-di-sarai near Muktsar, where his father had shifted back.

Guru Angad was married to **Mata Khirji** in January 1520 and had two sons, **Dasuji** and **Datuji**, and two daughters, **Amroji** and **Anokhiji**. The whole family had to leave their ancestral village when Mughal emperor Babur's army ransacked it.

Once Lehna heard the recitation of Guru Nanak's hymn from Bhai Jodhaji and was thrilled. He decided to go to Kartarpur to have a glimpse of Guru Nanak at the time of his ritual pilgrimage to Jwalamukhi temple, which he visited every year with his mother to worship Goddess Durga. He was completely transformed after meeting Guru Nanak and became his disciple. His devotion to the holy mission of Guru Nanak was so deep that he was made the second Guru on September 7, 1539 and was given a new name **Guru Angad Sahib** by Nanak himself.

After the death of Guru Nanak, Guru Angad shifted to Khadur Sahib village near Goindwal Sahib and carried forward the legacy of Guru Nanak, both in letter and spirit. Saints of different sects visited him and held detailed discussions about Sikhism with him.

Guru Angad introduced a new script *Gurmukhi*, modifying the old Punjabi script's characters. Very soon it was accepted by the masses. He took great interest in the education of children by opening many schools and thereby encouraged literacy. He started the tradition of *Mall Akhara* for the young where they were given physical and spiritual lessons. He wrote the biography of Guru Nanak with the help of Bhai Balaji and composed 63 *Slokas* that are included in the *Guru Granth Sahib*. Moreover, he popularised and expanded the institution of *Guru ka langar*.

Guru Angad visited all the important places established by Guru Nanak and he himself established hundreds of new *sangats* for preaching Sikhism. He was so popular that the Mughal ruler Humayun, after his defeat by Sher Shah Suri, came to seek the blessings of Guru Angad to regain the Delhi throne.

Following the example of his Guru, Guru Angad nominated Guru Amar Das as his successor and the third Guru, before he breathed his last on March 29, 1552, at the age of 48. Guru Angad led the Sikhs well during a period of great turmoil and established a separate religious identity for Sikhs.

III. Guru Amar Das

Guru Amar Das was born at Basarke village in Amritsar district on May 5, 1479. His father **Tej Bhan Bhalla** and mother **Bhalet Kaur** were religious people. They belonged to an orthodox Hindu family and paid annual visits to the sacred river Ganga at Haridwar. His mother is also known as **Sulakhani Devi** and **Laxmi Devi**.

Guru Amar Das was married to **Mata Mansa Deviji** and had four children: two sons, **Mohaji** and **Mohriji**, and two daughters, **Bibi Daniji** and **Bibi Bhaniji**. His second daughter Bibi Bhaniji was married to Guru Ram Das.

It is said that once Guru Angad's daughter, Bibi Amroji, sang hymns of Guru Nanak. Amar Das heard them and immediately went to Guru Angad. He became a devout disciple and served the Guru with all his strength and consciousness. He lived with Guru Angad at Khadur Sahib. He brought water for the Guru's bath and wood for *Guru ka langar*.

Guru Amar Das was appointed the third Guru in March 1552 at the age of 73. He established his headquarters at the newly built Goindwal. From here, he propagated Sikhism with meticulous planning and rare devotion. The Sikh *sangat* area was divided into 22 *manjis* as preaching centres. Each *manji* was under the charge of a devout Sikh. Guru Amar Das sent Sikh missionaries to different parts of India and himself visited most of them.

It is said that Emperor Akbar once went to meet Guru Amar Das. The emperor had to eat coarse rice with others in the *langar* before he could meet the Guru. He was so impressed by the system that he wished to grant royal property for *Guru ka langar*, which was humbly declined by the Guru. As a result, Akbar developed immense respect for the Guru. Even Guru Amar Das maintained cordial relations with Akbar. He persuaded Akbar to waive off pilgrim's tax – a toll for non-Muslims when crossing the sacred rivers Ganga and Yamuna.

Guru Amar Das was against the *purdah* (veil) system and *sati*. He advocated re-marriage of widows. He introduced new birth, marriage and death ceremonies. He fixed the *Guruparbs* for Sikhs to celebrate. They are *Deepawali*, *Vaisakhi* and *Maghi*. Visiting Hindu pilgrimage sites and paying tributes at Muslim places were prohibited for Sikhs.

Guru Amar Das had a *baoli* (water reservoir) constructed at Goindwal Sahib with 84 steps and declared it a Sikh pilgrimage. He composed either 709 or 869 hymns and verses (there is uncertainty over the exact figure), which are now part of the *Sri Guru Granth Sahib*.

His daughter Bibi Bhaniji and her husband Guru Ram Das had the true spirit of service and keen understanding of Sikh principles. Naturally, he appointed his son-in-law as his successor.

Guru Amar Das passed away at the ripe age of 95 on September 1, 1574 at Goindwal.

IV. Guru Ram Das

Jethaji, later Guru Ram Das, was born at Chuna Mandi in Lahore on September 24, 1534. He was a very handsome and promising child. His father **Baba Hari Dasji** and mother **Mata Daya Kaur**, however, were very poor and could not even ensure a proper meal for the child. They died when he was just seven years old. He was then forced to sell boiled gram to survive. He continued the practice even when he received shelter from Guru Amar Das, who brought him to Goindwal Sahib.

A regular participant in the religious congregation, he devoted most of his time in the development of Goindwal Sahib. He was married to the daughter of Guru Amar Das, **Bibi Bhaniji**, who bore him three sons: **Prithvi Chandji**, **Madhavji** and the legendary **Guru Arjun Dev**. Guru Ram Das was famous for 'his piety, devotion, energy and eloquence'. Capable in every respect, he was duly inducted as the fourth Guru on September 1, 1574.

Guru Ram Das laid the foundation stone of Ramdaspur, now famous as Amritsar. He started work on Santokhsar Sarovar but dropped the idea and concentrated on Amritsar Sarovar. Ramdaspur soon flourished and grew into a centre of international trade. He invited many merchants and artisans and helped them in making the place a pilgrimage for Sikhs. He introduced the *Masand* system in place of *Manji* and consolidated Sikh power. He introduced a new matrimonial system composed of *Four Lawans* to be recited at the time of marriage.

Guru Ram Das composed 638 hymns in *ragas* that are now part of SGGS. These include 246 *Padei*, 138 *Slokas*, 31 *Ashtpadis* and 8 *Vars*. He nominated his youngest son Arjun Dev as the fifth Guru. He then retired to Goindwal Sahib and passed away on September 1, 1581. He is remembered for the consolidation of Sikhism.

V. Guru Arjun Dev

Guru Arjun Dev was the youngest son of **Guru Ram Das** and **Mata Bhaniji**, born at Goindwal Sahib on April 15, 1563. Bhai Budhaji first taught him *Gurmukhi* and *Guruvani* and then he received proper education in Hindi, Sanskrit and Persian. A brilliant pupil, Arjun Dev had a sweet, mellifluous voice and sang hymns well. A perfect blend of devotion, sacrifice and humility, he married **Mata Gangaji** and had a son **Har Gobind Dev**, who later succeeded him as Guru.

Guru Arjun Dev was 18 years old when his father Guru Ramdas installed him as the fifth Guru. Thereafter, he worked diligently to spread and consolidate Sikhism.

Guru Arjun Dev completed two sacred *baolis* (tanks): Santokhsar and Amritsar. He had the foundation stone of Harmandir Sahib, Amritsar, laid by a Muslim saint Hazrat Mian Mirjee of Lahore in December 1588. After the completion of Harmandir Sahib, he founded the town of Tarn Taran Sahib near Goindwal Sahib and had a large Gurudwara constructed there. A deep and big sarovar was also dug and completed there. He also built a house for lepers in the true spirit of compassion.

He laid the foundation stone of yet another town named Kartarpur near Jalandhar city and had a large *baoli* constructed there. Mughal ruler Shah Jahan later destroyed this to construct a mosque there. The *baoli* was re-excavated under the alert eyes of Maharaja Ranjit Singh. However, it was destroyed once again by the Muslims some time thereafter.

Guru Arjun established Hargobindpur, a big town on the banks of a river, and constructed a very big and deep well for irrigation at Chheharta near Amritsar.

The most memorable and monumental work of Guru Arjun Dev is the compilation of *Sri Guru Granth Sahib* that was penned by Bhai Gurdasji. He himself contributed around two thousand verses to it. He had the *Adi Granth* installed at the Harmandir Sahib in September 1604. After its installation, Mughal emperor Akbar declared the *SGGS* as "the greatest Granth of synthesis".

Guru Arjun Dev was addressed as *Sachcha Patshah*. But the moment Jahangir became the Mughal emperor, there was a sudden change in the political and religious milieu. Jahangir was quite jealous of the Guru's fame, the growing number of the Sikhs and the spread of Sikhism.

Many false allegations were levelled against the Guru, one of which was helping the rebellious Khusro. He was subsequently tortured to death. Guru Arjun was made to sit on hot iron planks and burning sand was poured over his naked body. When his body was blistered, he was chained and thrown into the river Ravi. Thus Guru Arjun embraced martyrdom on May 30, 1606, just two years after the installation of the *Guru Granth Sahib*. Emperor Jahangir, in his autobiography, acknowledges that he personally ordered the execution of Guru Arjun.

It was a sad end for a great Guru, a positive thinker, a creative man and a peace-loving soul.

The life of Guru Arjun Dev will not be complete if some of his verses are not quoted. The following are two verses composed by the fifth Guru. One is an *Ashtapadi* and the other is *Sloka Sehskriti*:

1. *Sadh koi sang no kabahum dhavai.*

Ashtapadi: 1614

In the company of saints
The mind hankers not wildly,
In the company of saints
The soul attains happiness,
In the company of saints
Man gets a glimpse of the Invisible,
In the company of saints
Man endures the unbearable,
In the company of saints
Man reaches the height of spirit,
In the company of saints
Man stands in the Lord's presence,
In the company of saints
Man is aware only of the Lord,
In the company of saints
Man is granted His Name
Which is life's treasure,
Nanak is ever a sacrifice
Unto the living saints.

2. Saina sadh sarruh

Sloka Sehskriti: 202

The worry of saints is invincible
They are great warriors,
Humility is the metal plate over their breast,
Songs of the Lord's glory are their weapons,
Their buckles are the words of the Guru.
They ride the horses, chariots, and elephants of submission, love and compassion
And move through the divine path.
They advance towards the enemy fearlessly.
They sing the marching song of the Lord's praise
They conquer easily the five robber chiefs of sensuous pleasure
By conquering the senses
They feel and they actually conquer the whole world.

VI. Guru Har Gobind

The only son of **Guru Arjun Dev** and **Mata Gangaji** was born on June 19, 1595. He was extremely handsome, truly courageous and highly intelligent. He was married in about 1610 to **Mata Nanakiji**. He had a daughter called **Bibi Viroji** and five sons **Baba Gurdittaji, Suraj Malji, Ani Raiji, Atal Raiji** and **Tegh Bahadurji**. His first four sons passed away during the lifetime of the Guru and the only survivor, the fifth son, became the ninth Guru later in 1664. The life of Guru Har Govind was full of struggle and journeys, spiritual preaching and political strife. It was a tempestuous life of turmoil, activities and restlessness.

Just after the martyrdom of his father Guru Arjun Dev, he was nominated and installed as the sixth Guru in 1606 at the tender age of 11. The struggle for existence had taken the form of war, so there was no peace in the country. In accordance with the cruel wishes of the Mughal rulers, Muslim troops were torturing everyone. Sikhs had to keep swords and other weapons to save their lives. This was the time when Guru Har Gobind decided to wear two swords, one for *Piri* (spiritual enlightenment) and the other for *Miri* (military power). The physical and spiritual powers were blended well and the emergence of these "saint-soldiers" was regarded as essential and accepted wholeheartedly. The Guru himself learnt the adroit use of various weapons, as well as wrestling, riding and fighting, besides the favourite pastime, hunting. He advised Sikhs to take part in the military training and martial arts. All sorts of martial sports were introduced. He composed martial songs like *Vars*, which were sung daily to inculcate the fighting spirit in Sikh youth and inspire them to heroic deeds.

Within three years he made all efforts for safety and security. He had a wall erected around Amritsar and a *Lohgrah* constructed on its outskirts. *Akal Bunga* (Timeless Throne) or *Sri Akal Takht Sahib* was established just in front of the Golden Temple, Harmandir Sahib, in 1609.

Mughal emperor Jahangir could not tolerate the Sikh expansion, consolidation and militarisation on such a large scale. He imprisoned Guru Har Gobind in the Gwalior fort for three long years. Just after his release, on his request, 52 other prisoners were also released and he received the nickname *Bandi Chhor-Baba* (saint who freed the prisoners).

His *Dharma Prachar Yatras* (tours for spreading the religion) gave him immense power both in *Piri* and *Miri*. He raised an army and made Sikhism popular in different parts of the country.

The atmosphere was more vitiated when Shah Jahan became the Mughal ruler. As a result, Guru Har Gobind fought five battles during the reign of Shah Jahan and won all. After these successful encounters, he retired to Kartarpur but there too he had to wage war. Then he moved on to Kiratpur Sahib, where he established another Sikh centre. He spent around ten years of his life here and nominated his grandson Har Raiji as his successor and the seventh Guru.

On February 28, 1644 he breathed his last. When his body was on the pyre and the flames leapt high, many saint-soldiers tried to jump into the fire. Guru Har Rai stopped them. However, at least two of them were consumed by the fire along with the Guru.

VII. Guru Har Rai

Guru Har Rai was the son of **Baba Gurdittaji** and **Mata Nihal Kaur**, who was also popular as **Mata Anantiji**. The Guru was married to **Mata Krishan Kaur**, also known as **Sulakhaniji**. She was the daughter of Sri Daya Ramji of Bulandshahr in Uttar Pradesh. They had two sons, the elder was **Ram Raiji** and the younger **Har Krishan**, who later became the eighth Guru.

Guru Har Rai was installed as the seventh Guru on March 3, 1644. He loved peace and was against bloodshed. Though he maintained the new tradition of saint-soldiers, he never had any direct clash with the Mughal army and avoided any political controversy, barring two incidents. The Mughals once attacked his *Kafila*. His saint-soldiers fought bravely and defeated them.

The other incident relates to the Mughal's internal war of succession. It is claimed that he helped Dara Shikoh, the eldest son of Emperor Shah Jahan, escape from the bloody hands of Aurangzeb's ruthless troops. The Guru may have had a soft corner for Dara as he had saved his life on the request of Emperor Shah Jahan when he was seriously ill and others were unable to cure him. This was quite possible because the Guru had started an Ayurvedic Herbal Medical Hospital and research centre at Kiratpur Sahib.

In order to consolidate the influence of the Sikhs and acquire first-hand information, the Guru travelled far and wide and established as many as 360 new *manjis*. He faced all difficulties with courage and intelligence. He was true to the tradition of the Gurus, and did not meet his elder son Ram Raiji for the rest of his life when the latter tried to change the meaning of a couplet to please the Mughal emperor. He gave strict instructions to the Sikhs against making any changes in the original verse of the *Guru Granth Sahib* or the basic concepts or conventions set up by Guru Nanak Dev.

Guru Har Rai installed his younger son Har Krishan as the eighth Nanak and departed for heaven on October 6, 1661 at Kiratpur Sahib.

VIII. Guru Har Krishan

The younger son of **Guru Har Rai** and **Mata Krishan Kaurji** was named Har Krishan – a combination of the names of both his father and mother. Born on

July 7, 1656, he was the youngest to be declared Guru at around just five in 1661 before the departure of Guru Har Rai. This angered Guru Har Rai's elder son, Ram Rai. Out of sheer jealousy, he complained to Aurangzeb, who issued orders through Raja Jai Singh for the young Guru to appear before him.

Along with a few of his family members, he went to Delhi where he was received with honour by Raja Jai Singh and the Sikhs of Delhi. People from all walks of life came to pay a visit and have a glimpse of the youngest Guru. It is mentioned that Prince Muzzam also paid a visit.

At that moment, an epidemic of cholera and smallpox broke out in Delhi. The young Guru moved through all the affected areas and attended to sufferers of all castes and creeds. The Hindus, Muslims and Sikhs were impressed by the compassion, kindness and fearlessness shown by the inexperienced Guru. He was rightly named *Bal Pir* (child prophet).

The epidemic did not spare the child prophet. High fever and the dangerous smallpox struck him. His mother came to assist him but it was too late. Asked to name the next Guru, he repeatedly exclaimed '*Baba Bakala*' – which meant Tegh Bahadur, a resident of village Bakala, near the river Beas.

His end quickly drew near. He asked that nobody should mourn his death. He instructed them to sing hymns from *Guru Vani*. Too young to resist the combined attack of fever and smallpox, he breathed his last on March 30, 1664, slowly reciting the word '*Wahe Guru*'.

IX. Guru Tegh Bahadur

The last and only surviving son of **Guru Har Gobind** and **Mata Nanakiji**, Tegh Bahadur was born on April 1, 1621. His original name was Tyag Mal but the Sikhs began calling him Tegh Bahadur after he fought bravely and used his sword in a devastating manner in the battle of Kartarpur.

As a child, he preferred to meditate and his inner longing for meditation continued till the end. He always led a secluded life although he travelled a lot and kept meeting people. He actively participated in philosophical discourses to perfect his will and enrich his inner self. He had regular schooling and proper education, learning classical, vocal and instrumental music. He also had lessons in *Guru Vani* and Hindu mythology. A trained warrior, he had military training in swordsmanship, shooting, javelin throwing and horse riding.

He was married to **Mata Gujriji** at the early age of 15 on September 14, 1632. Mata Gujriji was the daughter of a rich and nobleman Lal Chand and Bishan Kaur of Kartarpur. She amply exhibited nobility through her disciplined behaviour and modest temperament. They had a son **Gobind Singh**, who later became the tenth and last living Guru of the Sikhs.

From 1644 to 1666, he spent 20 years in a house specially constructed for him by Bhai Mehra. Guru Har Krishan symbolically appointed him his successor by saying only 'Baba Bakala' before his premature death. Naturally, there was a hue and cry about it but after the declaration of Makhan Shah, "*Guru ladho re, Guru ladho re,*" most Sikhs accepted him. Under the leadership of Dhir Mal, however, some people attacked him and a bullet hit Guru Sahib. But he forgave all.

This was the time of Muslim cruelty against non-Muslims. Temples, gurudwaras and *baolis* were destroyed and mosques erected to replace them. But the Guru showed much patience, although he was arrested at Agra in June 1670, he was released soon and reached Anandpur Sahib again in 1671. After two years of rest, he again went on a long tour, had trees planted, tanks dug and sarovars constructed with *kar seva* (free service). He established important preaching centres at many places and returned to Anandpur Sahib.

He protested against the massacre of *Pandits* by Aurangzeb and, in 1675, decided to sacrifice himself for the cause of righteousness. First he installed his son Gobind Singh as the tenth Guru and then moved towards Delhi. Along with his prominent followers, he was arrested near Ropar. Kept in a prison at Bassi Pathanan, the Guru was tortured daily but he remained calm. He was offered freedom if he embraced Islam, which he refused. Then a *jallad* (executioner) was asked to sever his head. The order was implemented on November 11, 1675. Gurudwara Sis Ganj at Chandni Chowk in Old Delhi is mute proof of the cremation of the Sis (head). His body was burnt along with the house and belongings of Sikh Lakhi Shah Lubana. This place is now known as Gurudwara Rakab Ganj in New Delhi.

Guru Tegh Bahadur had composed *Guru Vani* in 15 *ragas*, apart from 57 *slokas*, which are a part of the SGGS. He is immortal as a poet, saint, Guru and martyr.

X. Guru Gobind Singh

Gobind Singh Sodhi is popularly known as Guru Gobind Singh. He was the tenth and last human teacher of the Sikh faith and thereafter declared the end of Guruship.

Guru Gobind Singh was born on December 22, 1666 at Patna in Bihar. The place where he was born and spent his childhood is in Patna city area. A big, sacred shrine called Takht Sri Harmandir Sahib now stands there, popularly called Patna Sahib. It is the throne or *takht* for Sikhs and one of the five most honoured seats of religious authority, now a Sikh pilgrimage.

In 1672 he was escorted to Chakk Nanki, another seat famous as Anandpur Sahib. There he received proper education that included reading and writing Punjabi (*Gurmukhi*), Hindi, Sanskrit and Persian.

Guru Gobind Singh was formally installed as the tenth Guru on November 11, 1675, a black day on which Guru Tegh Bahadur was beheaded. That extraordinary, unforgettable day was indelibly imprinted in the mind of the innocent and inexperienced Guru. He understood the need to be *Pir* and *Mir* simultaneously to save the Sikhs. It is evident in his early poems. His first poetic composition, *Var Sri Bhagautiji Ki*, known as *Chandi di Var*, depicts in detail the well-known contest of gods and demons represented by Goddess Chandi or Durga and Mahishasur according to *Durga Saptashati* and *Markandeya Purana.* He developed this theme of spirituality and divinity being protected and saved by weapons. This was an unannounced declaration of prolonged battle against injustice, tyranny and demonic acts.

Guru Gobind Singh founded Paonta on the banks of the river Yamuna and shifted there in April 1685. During his stay there, he composed most of his poems, through which he preached love and equality, and a strict moral code of conduct.

He wielded the sword as a means of manliness and self-respect, to be used only in self-defence, as a last resort. He declared:

When all other means have failed,
It is but lawful to take to the sword.

To hone his martial skills, he regularly practised riding, swimming, archery and fencing.

"Arms are essential to safeguard the scriptures," so said Parashuram.

"The fight between the gods and the demons is a sport for the Almighty, who Himself beholds the sport," claimed Guru Gobind Singh in *Chandi Charita Ukata Bilas*:

The Eternal, Limitless, Indescribable, Infinite
Timeless, Formless, Indefinable, Imperishable Being
Who generated the spirit and energy.
Gave the four *Vedas*,
Brought into existence three qualities:
***Sattva, Rajas, Tamas* (Truth, Motion, Passivity)**
Pervades all the three parts of the Universe
Who created the day and night.
With the Sun and Moon as Eyes,
Having manifested five elements
Who created the Beautiful World.

Sheesh Mahal Sahib (Punjab)

Gurudwara Bangla Sahib
(New Delhi)

Having spread enmity between the gods and demons,
He prompts them to fight
And then having seated Himself,
He beholds the sport.

Guru Gobind Singh established a direct relationship with his disciples. He called them *Khalsa*. It was he who created a militant body in Sikhism to counter tyrants and be an active participant in that eternal sport known as 'the struggle for existence'.

The Guru gave the Khalsa a concrete form on March 20, 1699 when a large number of Sikhs had gathered for the annual festival of Baisakhi. It was done in a dramatic manner to test the Sikhs' courage and dedication, and for the selection of leaders. The Guru appeared before the crowd with a naked sword. According to the description given by Koer Singh, the Guru asked: "Is there present a true Sikh who would offer his head to the Guru as sacrifice?" After a minute of tense silence, he repeated the call. At the third call, Daya Ram from Lahore rose and followed the Guru into a tent.

After two minutes, the Guru appeared with the sword soaked in fresh blood. He repeated the same question. This time Dharam Das from Hastinapur rose and followed the Guru inside the enclosure. The Guru then reappeared, repeated the question and one by one took three other Sikhs – Mukham Chand from Dwarka, Himmat from Jagannathpur and Sahib Chand from Karnataka – inside to sacrifice their heads. All they had to give was their life – but their heads were saved.

When they finally re-emerged from the tent, they were metamorphosed both in outer appearance and inner essence. They were "dressed in saffron coloured raiment topped over neatly tied turbans of the same colour with swords dangling by their sides". They were declared to be the *Panj Piare*, the five devoted disciples beloved to the Guru. These five formed the nucleus of a self-abnegating, martial and casteless fellowship of the Khalsa.

They were all given the surname 'Singh', meaning 'lion', and required to henceforth wear the five symbols of the Khalsa, all beginning with the letter 'K':

Kesh – long hair and beard

Kangha – a comb in the kesh to keep it tidy

Kara – a steel bracelet

Kachcha – short breeches

Kirpan – a dagger

The Khalsa were given the duty to help the 'helpless' and fight against the 'oppressor'. In accordance with this, the Guru himself changed his name from Gobind Rai to Gobind Singh.

His enemies did not take kindly to this and attacked Anandpur. After sporadic battles, the Guru's strength was reduced to three Sikhs with whom he escaped to Malwa. In the struggle, his two sons Ajit Singh and Jujhar Singh were killed. In a conspiracy, his other two sons Jorawar Singh and Fateh Singh were captured and executed on December 13, 1705.

Then Guru Gobind Singh sent his famous letter *Zafarnama* to Aurangzeb, but to no avail. In a fierce battle on December 29, 1705, he was greatly helped by

Mai Bhago and her 40 Sikh soldiers, who died during the battle. They were blessed as 40 *Mukte*, **the saved ones**. The place is called Muktsar – *the pool of liberation*.

After a month, he arrived at Talwandi, famous as Damdama Sahib. In a conspiracy, Guru Gobind Singh was attacked while resting in his chamber and severely injured. Though the attackers were killed, the injury proved fatal. Many expert surgeons treated him, including an Englishman Dr Cole, sent by Emperor Bahadur Shah. The wound aggravated however, and the stitches were opened. There was profuse bleeding which weakened the Guru. Eventually, he departed for the heavenly abode on October 7, 1708.

XI. Guru Granth Sahib

On Wednesday, the day of *Budh* (Mercury), October 6, 1708, Guru Gobind Singh respectfully placed the *Sri Guru Granth Sahib* before the big gathering and offered five paise and a coconut, then bowed his head and announced before the *Sangat*: "It is my commandment: Own the *Sri Granthiji* in my place. He who so acknowledges it will obtain his rewards. The Guru will rescue him. Know this as the Truth."

Thereby the Guruship and succession was passed over to the Holy Book, *Sri Guru Granth Sahib*, with due respect and ceremony. This was the end of the line of human Gurus.

Guru Gobind Singh declared: "The Guru's spirit will henceforth be in the *Granth* and the Khalsa. Where the *Granth* is with any five Sikhs representing the Khalsa, there will be the Guru. The Gurus and disciples alike have always revered the word enshrined in the Holy Book.

The word is of Divine Origin. It has one day to take the place of the Guru."

When Guru Gobind Singh declared the *Sri Guru Granth Sahib* as his successor, it made the SGGS immortal. The Holy Book has become the Guru of the Sikhs for all time to come. It is this faith that is all – be it in the *Formless Nirgun Absolute* who is in every being and action or in the form of the *Sagun Guru Granth Sahib*, which speaks not but tells all, guides all and saves all. Now the *Sri Guru Granth Sahib* is the Eternal Guru.

In the words of Dr S. Radhakrishnan: "We find in the *Adi Granth* a wide range of mystical emotion, intimate expression of the personal realisation of God and rapturous hymns of divine love. The Sikh creed includes belief in the ten Gurus and the *Adi Granth*."

ꝏ

Modern Intellectuals On Guru Nanak

1. "At a time when men were conscious of failure, Nanak appeared to renovate the spirit of religion and humanity. He did not found a new faith or organise a new community. That was done by one of his successors, notably the fifth Guru. Nanak tried to build a nation of self-respecting men and women, devoted to God and their leaders, filled with a sense of equality and brotherhood for all."

   Dr S. Radhakrishnan
   Adi Granth and the Sikh Religion

2. "Nanak belongs to the galaxy of mystics which this land has seen, in unbroken succession, since the time of the rishis of the *Vedas*."

   V. Raghavan
   Nanak – His Tradition and Thought

3. "Punjab was also the soil which gave birth to what Toynbee describes as 'a monument of creative spiritual intercourse between the two traditional religions whose relations have otherwise not been happy'. This

monument, the *Sikh Panth*, owes its origin to Nanak who had travelled up to Mecca and who expressly declares himself as a prophet of the harmony of the two religions."

V. Raghavan
The Saint Singer of India

4. "Guru Nanak was the spectator of all time and all existence."

Dharmant Singh
The Perfumed Radiance of Sri Guru Nanak

5. "Guru Nanak came out with his message of fraternity and equality. He had a liberal mind. Guru Nanak attempted to lead men to the noble path of goodness and virtue. He kindled the flame of love and sympathy in the minds of millions of people."

K P Keshav Menon
In Search of God

6. "The Name is mysterious concrete embodiment, as it were, of the deity, and the power of the Guru lies in that he can convey it to the seekers. And he only can convey it."

Dr Macnicol
Indian Theism

7. "But Guru Nanak was not a visionary idealist or a speculative theorist. He preached no complicated philosophy couched in the unintelligible language of the other worldly people. He was a practical man – one with the men of this world. He spoke to the people in the language of the people and explained his ideas to them with examples drawn from everyday common life.

Ganda Singh
Guru Nanak's Impact on History

8. "It would be difficult to point to a religion of greater originality than that of Guru Nanak."

Macauliffe
The Sikh Religion

9. "Nanak was a man, the like of whom is yet to be known to the history of mankind; a man whose life opened an era in the history of India and Asia – in the history of humanity.... At rare intervals in history doth appear a man like Nanak."

Sadhu T L Vaswani
A Prophet of the People

10. "Guru Nanak is widely known and highly respected as a prophet, a seer, a saviour, a redeemer, a divine master and a spiritual preceptor. He enjoyed so much of reverence and popularity even in his own lifetime that his name became a legend, both at home and abroad. The religious minded of his own country and community, calling him *Nanak Dev* and interpreting *Dev* as 'God', considered him God-on-Earth or an *Avatar*: an incarnation of God. He was acclaimed as *Pir-i-Hind* in the Muslim world."

Harnam Singh Shan
Guru Nanak as a Man

11. "Guru Nanak's thought cannot be made to conform to the categories of *Advaita* doctrine.... The total range of Guru Nanak's thought makes this equation manifestly impossible and accordingly requires us to reject the monistic alternative."

Will McLeod
Guru Nanak and the Sikh Religion

12. "He (Guru Nanak) was not merely a founder of a faith but he was a world teacher and a philosopher

and above all, a great social reformer.

Guru Nanak was a many faceted personality – a mystic, saint, poet and reformer.

Guru Nanak was neither a fanatic nor a bigot. He laid stress on the fundamental truth in all religions.

Guru Nanak was practical to the core, and he never preached what he did not practise.

Guru Nanak was a person of extraordinary moral courage and independence."

Ujjal Singh
Guru Nanak – A Social Revolutionary

13. "The significance of Guru Nanak for our people and our history is that appearing at a time when ideas about the religious life, morality and ideals which must guide the human community, had sunk to an extreme level of obscurantism, he enunciated the eternal, principle of the worship of the One, Uncreated, Eternal, Absolute, who is not confined within the restricting forms of creeds. To this divine reality he gave names which were not redolent of this or that tradition only, but come from sources Muslim as much as Hindu, Yogic or others. As against the monastic ideal of indifference to the temporal reality, he sought to make soul-awakened man stationed amid moral duty in the spirit of devotion and service.... Hence he called upon the people and their leaders to abjure the path of pursuing the lower objectives and to hitch their souls to the highest of objectives (*Parmatma*) which brings joy in this life and emancipation (*Moksha*), which is the supreme goal of life."

Gurbachan Singh Talib
Guru Nanak – An Outline of his Teachings

14. "It was he who exposed the hollowness of empty ritualism long before any of these appeared in the field. The supreme importance of purity of character, concentration of thought; sincerity of devotion and above all dedicating one's life to the alleviation of the sufferings of one's fellow beings was emphasised by Guru Nanak towards the close of the fifteenth century."

Biman Behari Majumdar
Guru Nanak and his Contemporaries

15. "In calling God the Creator, Guru Nanak differs from all the six schools of Indian philosophy.... Guru Nanak, on the other hand, asserts that the Supreme Reality is the Creator of the universe, both animate and inanimate."

Dr Bhai Jodh Singh
Guru Nanak's Concept of God

16. "Despite its special characteristics, Sikhism was not exotic in India's religious life, it was a peculiar expression of the *Bhakti* movement which swept over practically the whole of India; and it derived inspiration and vigour from the perennial spring of India's spiritual traditions. What Guru Nanak aimed at was not a socio-religious cataclysm; his purpose was to remove the abuses that had crept into the old order and set it right by restating it, in terms of newer environments. The Guru reviewed the religious problem of his day as one of adjustment and simplification; he was a rebel indeed, but not one who insisted upon extermination."

Dr Anil Chandra Banerji
Background of Guru Nanak's Teachings

17. "Guru Nanak preached these ideas not to one sect or community but to men of all races, of all colours, of all countries and, shall we say, for all times, because the truths he laid bare will never be changed and will never be found wanting to satisfy the seeker's quests."

Sher Singh
Guru Nanak: A World Teacher

18. "Guru Nanak did more than other *Bhakt* saints. He showed not only a deep insight into the malady that was corroding Hindu society but also a rare boldness and courage to prescribe the radical cure. Others had said that a *grihastha*, a householder, could lead a saintly life but they themselves lived a life of renunciation. Nanak showed by example that it was so."

Jayalal Kaul
Guru Nanak – De-brahmanising Hinduism

19. "Guru Nanak was a messenger of goodwill and peace. He was an embodiment of communal harmony. His noble teachings have influenced the religious, social and political thoughts of millions of people of India and abroad."

Abdul Majid Khan
Muslim Devotees of Guru Nanak

20. "In his famous *Japji*, he (Guru Nanak) has described five stages of mental and spiritual development of the individual in this world. To begin with, a seeker of truth must develop a scientific outlook. He must study and enter into the realm of the Laws of Nature – *Dharma Khand* – and see that in this universe nothing happens haphazardly. There are systems and laws, wider laws covering the smaller laws and so on. After having a deep-rooted conviction in the

systematic working of the universe, he must acquire an artistic vision and enter the realm of reflection – *Gyan Khand.* He must convince himself of his being next to nothing by imagining the vastness and endlessness of God's becomings. Having developed a scientific outlook and an artistic insight, he should cultivate a creative attitude and enter the Realm of Beauty – *Saram Khand*:

Saram Khand ki bani roop,
Tithai gharat ghariai bahut anoop.

Thus a man who remains just a creature and does not create – a crop or a table, a poem or a pot – wastes his life like a worm.

When the seeker of truth has successfully covered the first three stages, then he is eligible to enter the remaining two Realms – *Karam Khand* and *Sach Khand* – the Realm of Grace and the Realm of Truth.

Giving up egocentricity he prays for the Grace of God, which makes him a hero who identifies his own good with the good of others. He now overcomes distinctions of me and mine and thee and thine. He merges himself into the real and the true and thus becomes a citizen of the Realm of Truth, where, by the Grace of God, he finds enjoyment in everything and happiness everywhere."

Nanak nadri nadar nihal

Sher Singh
Guru Nanak: A World Teacher

21. "Guru Nanak was, no doubt, a symbol of the process of eternal spiritual revival. He recognised the prophets

of the past of all lands and he gave his message of truth to his countrymen in particular and to the whole world in general."

Akhtar Ahmad Qrainvi
Symbol of Unity

22. "Guru Nanak was not only a great poet and an accomplished saint but also a revolutionary in his social conduct and a supporter of equality between men. The value of a man should be judged not by his wealth or breed, nor by his knowledge, but by the purity of his heart and the spotless nobility of his deeds. This was his teaching which he did not only preach but also practised."

Ramdhari Singh Dinkar
Guru Nanak and Indian Sadhna

23. "The main thought currents of Nanak were not much different from the fundamental ideology of Kabir, nor was there any vast mentionable difference between the methods of *Sadhna* favoured by Nanak and the *Sahaj-Sadhna* of Kabir. But there was, undoubtedly, a difference between the ways in which they worked – a difference by which even their *Vanis* could not remain uninfluenced."

Parsuram Chaturvedi
Contribution of Guru Nanak to Saint Literature

24. "Guru Nanak is to me one of the most attractive and significant figures in Indian history – one of a long succession of teachers from Manu, the great law-giver, Vedvyas, the epic poet, Buddha, the wise one, Shankara, the prince of reasoning, and then Nanak – the great synthesiser."

Ram K Vepa
Guru Nanak: The Great Synthesiser

25. "Nanak was a great teacher in this long process of national integration – wise, gentle and compassionate, no man drew more from the wisdom of India and no man in turn gave more to the common pool to serve as an inspiration to generations, long afterwards."

Ram K Vepa
Guru Nanak: The Great Synthesiser

26. "Nanak was perhaps the foremost among those who, while condemning the blind adherence to tradition, upheld the supremacy of moral values in everyday life. He preached truth and humility that are the virtues of the divine. He was the cultural leader not only of his followers but of the whole of India."

Satya Narayan Sinha
Introduction to Guru Nanak

27. "Guru Nanak was born at a time when our people were torn apart into groups drawn against one another. He laboured to join them into one league of love in the service of God and mankind. Through stirring words and songs he called on people to regard all religions as equal, to make no difference between Hindu and Muslim, between man and woman, between the mighty and the meek, between one caste and another.

    Guru Nanak belongs to all of us, and his teaching is one of our priceless treasures."

Mrs Indira Gandhi
In a message on 8.10.69

28. "Guru Nanak spent all his life preaching persistently and with sincerity in a very simple language these basic things to the people which enlighten the mind

and purify the heart and make a person a man of God and show him the correct path in life."

Dr Zakir Hussain
Message of Guru Nanak

29. "Like the true Vedantic, Nanak has declared God to be both far and near and gives an assurance to devotees that God would remove their sorrows.... Guru Nanak lays great stress on the right type of purity, internal purity, and not the external purity of the body."

M A Karandikar
Guru Nanak: His Life and a Comparative Study

30. "Whether Nanak was acquainted with Christian truth is a debated question, but whether he was or not, we must allow that, being in the same degree conversant with the Mohammedan faith, he may have known something of the revelation of God – His Word, the true teacher, God incarnate, the Lord Jesus Christ."

J W Youngson
Encyclopaedia of Religion and Ethics

31. "Man's approach to God was Nanak's main concern. He rejects as utterly useless the pilgrimage and penance, superstition and sacrifice, discussion and discourse. These are not the means to commune with the divine, to attain inner peace or to still the inner hunger. According to him the 'real life is a life within us', and spiritual communion necessarily internal.... Nanak speaks of 'walking in the Master's command' (*Hukumi vajayi chalna*) and this sums up his teaching.

S K Ramchandra Rao
Nanak: The Mystic

∞

The Need of Nanak

In *Hindi*, *Brij Bhasha* and *Gurmukhi* there are many *sakhis* – small didactic songs – about the life of Guru Nanak. They are known as *Janam Sakhis* or biographical takes in poetry. They contain details about Guru Nanak and his associates and throw adequate light on small but important incidents related to the Guru. In one such *sakhi*, the previous life of Nanak is described. According to this, King Janak, the father of Sita, took rebirth as Guru Nanak.

> ***The sakhi says that once King Janak, along with Dharmaraj, went on a visit to hell. He saw the miserable condition of the inmates there. Aggrieved at their plight, his heart was filled with pain and a sense of renunciation. On account of the noble deeds of the king, many sinners received salvation when he asked that they should be freed. However, he was advised that they would all have to go to Earth for their emancipation. To purify them and make them lead a pious life, the king was therefore reborn as Guru Nanak.***

Modern man may not take this mythological story as true but the fact is that during his lifetime, Nanak saved millions of humans from committing sins and indulging in worldly vices. He raised his voice against social malpractices, immoral acts, religious crimes and spiritual degeneration. He spoke against the crimes of the wealthy, sins of men, injustice by rulers and excesses by their men.

Those who have faith in him consider that it was the need of the time that Nanak came to help others and spread equality, fraternity and oneness.

World in Flames

It's a hell-like situation in the world. The whole world is burning. The flames of hatred are spreading fast, with each country and each community affected. The problems of pollution and global warming are growing. As a result, glaciers in Antarctica and other places are melting and the water level of the Atlantic Ocean is steadily rising. All these are threats to the very existence of the earth and life on it.

On the other hand, all of us are cutting trees foolishly and living beings are dying because of pollution. Nations and various terrorist organisations are seeking nuclear weapons that can be used for mass destruction. There are enough stockpiles of nuclear weapons to destroy the earth many times over.

The production, demand and consumption of medicines are at peak levels. The general health of people has deteriorated, thanks to unhealthy food, polluted air, water and unnatural living conditions.

Gurudwara Sis Ganj Sahib (Delhi)

Five articles of faith distinguish a Sikh and are essential for preserving life ...
1. Kesh; 2. Kangha; 3. Kara; 4. Kachcha; 5. Kirpan

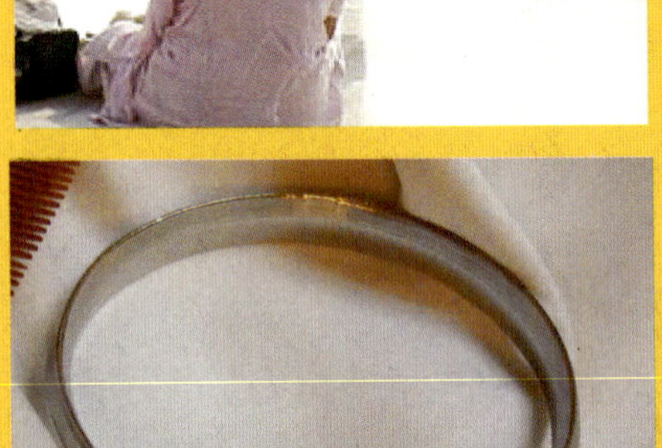

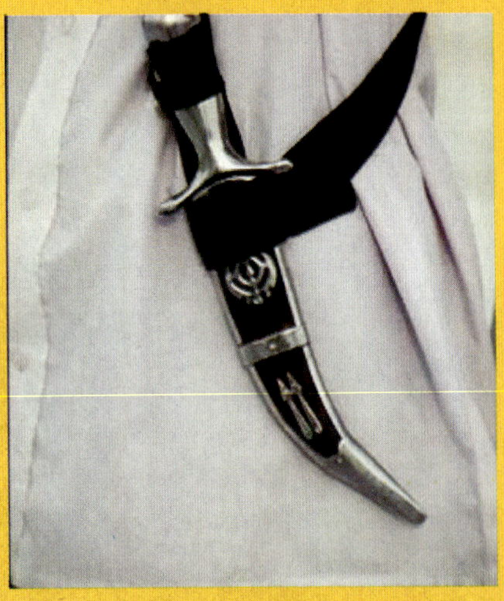

Panj Pyare (the five beloved ones)
— Bestowing of Guruship on Khalsa Panth

Man, the most sublime creation of Nature, has forgotten the purpose of his existence. This beautiful planet is fast turning into a deathtrap. So, a Nanak is the most urgent need of the present times.

Saving Humanity

Nanak is needed to purify minds, objects and elements; to make people think and work in the right direction; to make them feel equality, fraternity, love and compassion so that they forget enmity, hatred, lust and cruelty; so that the eternal, formless God can replace the modern god of money and materialism; so that man can work honestly for inner piety and universal welfare, instead of accumulating wealth solely for selfish purposes.

Nanak is needed for the emancipation of all – the brave and the meek, the high and the low, the rich and the poor; for salvation and deliverance, so that the entire world can be a better place to live in, with peace and happiness all around. Now, more than ever before, the moral and ethical values that Guru Nanak preached and practised are required to deliver the world from the path of death, destruction and doom.

ꝏ

Guru Nanak's Ways of Worship

Guru Nanak was a rare devotee and worshipper who himself was a renowned and most acceptable Guru. He said that only a Guru could show the real path to God. He himself had God for his Guru, and God was the Guru *par excellence* since God and Nature are the fountainhead of all knowledge and "the primary teacher". Patanjali takes God to be the oldest teacher, which Nanak confirms: "*The Guru of Gurus is but One.*"

Without the true Guru none has found God, and God had put Himself into the true Guru. In keeping with the great tradition, Nanak declares, "The Guru is Shiva, the Guru is Vishnu and Brahma. The Guru is the Mother Goddess."

Nanak was so determined and eager to be closer to God that he followed all the popular and successful ways to reach Him fast. He saw, learnt and tested all the possible ways of worship in the spirit of a true Indian sage.

Sumiran

Smaran (remembering) and *Sumiran* (recitation) are perfect shortcuts to God, the Almighty for going closer to and feeling oneness with Him. Nanak claimed that those who do not remember the Lord are not alive or healthy. It's a waste of life for them to live without God.

With rare determination, he employed all ways of remembering the Lord. The ways of remembering are *Shravan* (listening to the name), *Smaran* (remembering the Name by oneself), *Sumiran* (to recollect the name) and *Kirtan* (to recite the name). Even one of these ways can easily ensure solace and satisfaction, closeness and intimacy, fullness and richness to man. Nanak believed that all names are His name. So, he willingly adopted many: *Nirankar, Kartar, Omkar, Ek Omkar, Pati, Satnam, Wahe Guru, Absolute, Supreme, Pita, Pritam, Khasam, Nam, Baba Bhai, Piara, Sukhsagar, Anjana, Swambhu, Manmohan, Sakha, Amar, Hukumi, Shahanshah, Prabhu, Sahib, Guru* and many more, including other *Sagun* incarnations.

Nanak himself had many names: Nanak Dev, Nanak Nath, Nanak Shah, Nanak Nirankari, Nirankari Baba Guru, Satguru, Wahe Guru, Jagat Guru, Baba, Shah Faqir, Baba Nanak, Faqir Aulia, Pir-i-Hind, Avatar Baba, Guru Baba, Hazrat Nanak, Guruparmeshwar, etc.

Bhavas

For Nanak, "*the body is the palace, the temple and the abode of God.*" He said the moment one turns towards his inner self and surrenders to Him, he feels the closeness and oneness, and is immersed in the warmth of the Lord's love. Nanak was ready to go to the Lord in any mood, at any moment and treated Him as his friend, beloved and spouse. For him, *Atma-nivedana* or complete surrender to the Lord was important. Naturally, he displayed all the '*bhavas*' (moods).

In the mood of *Dasya bhava*, he is the slave of God: *"I am the servant and porter at Thy gate," "Nanak is His slave and even a sacrifice unto Him."* In the mood of a friend, *Sakha bhava*, he claims, "*I have no friend like God. There are no real friends but the Guru and God,*" and requests "*come my friend, that I may behold Thee,*" and has a word of advice for all, "*Pray to the Lord, to the True Guide that in Him thou may meet the beloved friend.*"

In *Madhur bhava*, the mood of lover and beloved, he uses the similes and metaphor of bride and bridegroom, in terms of a lady's love for her spouse or beloved. He feels that if *"she pleases not her spouse, all her preparations are in vain";* and he praises the women *"who has God for her spouse"*, for *"her Beloved is an abode of pleasure, ever young and true";* she is lucky for *"she knoweth no man but her beloved"*, and *"painful is the night for the young bride, without her beloved she sleepeth not". "Nanak saith, God alone is the spouse of all,"* so he says *"burn the arm that embraceth not the bridegroom"*. His advice to all is clear: all of us should seek *"the closeness of the Lord"*.

Sangats

The acceptance of all the common ways and popular names resulted in instant fame and respect. Whoever came to know him, liked him and wherever he went, he was revered. During his lifetime, the entire country looked up to him as a religious leader. He was not confined to Punjab and did not belong to the Sikhs only. His early *sangats* were at faraway places like Patna, Dhubri, Dacca and Nander. There was not a single Hindu in India who refused to bow before the Guru. His *sakhis* are taught in schools and colleges. Villagers sang his verses too, along with those of Kabir, Dadu and Ravidas.

Guru Nanak chose and propagated all ideas that he liked and considered useful for the masses. It was natural for him to adopt common ways of worshipping. It paid good dividends when he selected the musical way, which has been the core of worship as well as entertainment for Indians from time immemorial.

This world teacher was not confined to a particular region or sect:

Baba Nanak Shah Faqir,
Hindu ka Guru. Mussalman ka Pir.

It was but natural that his dead body vanished and only flowers remained. This was the best way, since those flowers were both cremated and buried.

Sisyas

He made many disciples, wherever he went. They were called *Sisya* in Hindi and *Sikh* in Punjabi. Later, all his disciples came to be known as *Sikhs*. Incidentally, all the first *panj piare* of Guru Gobind Singh hailed from outside Punjab. The Gurudwaras in other regions easily outnumber the ones in Punjab. Of the five most important pilgrimages of the Sikhs, four are outside Punjab.

Sagun and Nirgun

Nanak is acclaimed as the 'great synthesiser'. In the process of synthesising, a synthesiser gets mixed with all that he tries to synthesise. Nanak accepted other ideas and methods; in return he was accepted, liked and revered by others.

All his activities were directed towards service of the Lord via service of the masses. Through all these different ways of worship, Guru Nanak has expressed his own emotions towards the Lord. He accepted all, *dharma*, *artha*, *kama* and *moksha*, and rejected none. He neatly synthesised religions. He imperceptibly blended the *Vedas*, the *Brahma Sutra*, the *Upanishads* and the *Bhagwad Gita*. In all these he is closer to ***Bhartrihari***, who produced *Sringar Shatakam*, *Vairagya Shatakam* and *Niti Shatakam* to declare.

"Brahma is without beginning and end, whose essence is the word, which is the cause of the manifested phenomena, who appears as the objects from which the creation of the world proceeds."

Nanak said the same thing to his teacher: *"If you can worship the Nirankari God, who has neither end nor limit, then you can teach me."*

Guru's Ideals

Guru Nanak accepted and adopted all the means – human, divine and sublime – for a pious and pleasant life. That is why Bhai Gurdas claimed Nanak to be "the knower of all time and all space," and also '*Ek Omkar and Omkar*.'

Nanak was in favour of contemplation and meditation and says: "The divine mystery is revealed not through reading but through understanding."

He affirms the value of contemplation: "One may read throughout one's life, read even with every breath; yet of all things, it is only the contemplative life that really matters. All else is the fret and prattle of ego."

This does not mean he was against reading. On the contrary, he advocates: "As by lighting the lamp, darkness is dispelled, so by reading religious books, the mind is cleared of sins."

Guru Nanak stood at the centre of the ways of worship, accepting some and rejecting others. Whichever he accepted, he placed them at the helm and accepted these from the inner core of his heart. Whatever he rejected, he discarded into oblivion, as he rejected them with all his might. This is the main reason why Sikhism is a religion of strong beliefs and complete dedication, of exuberant energy and incessant indulgence.

His disciples have no time to rest except at night. Various engagements keep the continuous flow of their energy uninterrupted.

With his *Ek Omkar*, Guru Nanak supplied us the much-needed sap: eternal and blissful.